The Prac' Dementia Caregiver Guide

A Doctor's View on How to Overcome Behavioral Challenges, Enhance Communication, And Access Support While Ensuring Self-Care

Daily Blueprint for Busy Families

Sam Toroghi MD

Copyright © 2024 by Savvy Scrolls Publishing LLC

All rights reserved. No part of this publication may be reproduced, stored or transmitted in any form or by any means, electronic, mechanical, photocopying, recording, scanning, or otherwise without written permission from the publisher. It is illegal to copy this book, post it to a website, or distribute it by any other means without permission.

First edition

To my dearest Nila, whose light guides my endeavors and whose love gives purpose to these pages.

A Special GIFT for You!

As a token of my gratitude for purchasing this book, I am delighted to offer you a special gift.

"**Nourishing the Mind:** *A Caregiver's Guide to Diet and Nutrition for Dementia*" is an essential guide that offers expert nutritional advice to improve brain health. It focuses on optimal hydration and easy-to-swallow meals and provides numerous recipes tailored to meet the unique needs of dementia patients, boosting their cognitive function.

Scan the QR code below to Download your FREE copy now!

https://savvyscrolls.net/dementia

Table of Contents

Introduction 1
Part One: Awareness **6**
Chapter 1: What Is Dementia? 7
Chapter 2: Understanding the Stages 24
Chapter 3: A Different Perspective 38
Part Two: Action **52**
Chapter 4: The First Steps 53
Chapter 5: Adjusting Period 68
Chapter 6: Exploring Ways to Communicate 82
Chapter 7: Dealing With Challenging Days 94
Chapter 8: Finding Common Ground 116
Part Three: Assess **129**
Chapter 9: Understanding Your Role 130
Chapter 10: Taking Care of Yourself 146
Chapter 11: When It's Beyond Your Control 163
Conclusion 184
References 191

> *"To care for those who once cared for us is one of the highest honors."*
>
> **Tia Walker**

Introduction

Tyler was looking forward to spending part of the holiday break with his aunt. The first semester of college had been challenging, and he'd hoped to feed on more of the encouragement he'd first received when he was accepted into the school of his dreams. Tyler pulled into the driveway and opened the door to let himself in the same way he'd always done, but the greeting was different this time.

"Who are you? Why are you here? Get out of my house before I call the police!" Aunt Sheila yelled.

Shocked, Tyler replied, "Aunt Sheila, it's me!" Sheila ran towards her phone to call the police. Just then, her sister, Kendra, ran into the room to intercept the phone call. After calming things down, she asked Tyler to join her on the front porch, where she'd share the news.

"Your Aunt Sheila was diagnosed with dementia a month or so ago," Kendra said. "I knew she was 'slipping,' but I didn't know it was bad enough for you to have to be here full-time," said Tyler.

"You know me, always there to steer the ship," Kendra responded.

You're likely holding this book in your hand because in the wake of a dementia diagnosis, you're the one who has to steer the ship. You're officially a caregiver, and while most people are familiar with that word, not everyone is familiar with everything that it means. Before we delve into the specifics of this role, let's first explore some facts about your new reality.

- In 2020, 41.8 million Americans provided unpaid care to an adult over the age of 50.

- 89% of caregivers provide care for a relative or other loved one, such as a spouse.

- Caregivers provide an estimated $470 billion in free labor each year.

- Caregivers provide unpaid care to loved ones for an average of 4.5 years.

- Family caregivers who live with their senior relative spend an average of 37.4 hours a week on direct caregiving duties. Those who don't live with their relatives spend 23.7 hours a week on these duties.[1]

These statistics can be overwhelming, which is why dementia isn't something for a caregiver to shoulder alone. According to Sagepub.com, dealing with a dementia diagnosis and all that comes with it becomes more bearable when the patient's family is involved. Families and staff reach a shared understanding and become a unified voice for change, staff-to-family communication becomes stronger, and confidence and positive changes in the well-being of patients increase. Also, confidence in discussing dementia's trajectory and palliative care improves, and the patient more easily remembers family interactions.[2] Still, dementia seems to only be a taker. But when families share the burden, this togetherness can result in more positive outcomes than expected.

If you think everything is about to change because a loved one has dementia, you're right. The average life expectancy for someone diagnosed with the most common form of dementia is ten years, but the disease can last anywhere from

---

[1] Claire Samuels, "Caregiver Statistics: A Data Portrait of Family Caregiving in 2023," June 15, 2023, https://www.aplaceformom.com/senior-living-data/articles/caregiver-statistics.
[2] Jack Hayward et al., "Interventions Promoting Family Involvement With Care Homes Following Placement of a Relative With Dementia: A Systematic Review," *Dementia* 21, no. 2 (December 11, 2021): 618–47, https://doi.org/10.1177/14713012211046595.

2-26 years.[3] This means that life management can become increasingly more difficult for a long time. Fortunately, while the struggles are many, so are the resources for support. And the good thing is that you're not alone. The caregivers and physicians who came before you have created many resources to help you navigate your loved one's dementia. But information overload can be overwhelming!

Typically, once your loved one is diagnosed, the first thing you realize is how much you have to learn. You'll acquire a new vocabulary, read studies and recommendations, and throw yourself into message boards of real people with real experience to help you better understand your own situation. Because information is infinite on the internet, it's easy to get stuck in a rabbit hole of research. This guide will help you focus on the most critical aspects of dementia and the details of caregiving that apply to you right now. It will also help you stay informed and optimistic about the time you have left with your loved one instead of how time suddenly feels short.

The Practical Caregiver Dementia Guide is based on caregiving's "AAA Method," or the "Awareness, Action, Assess Method." Part One will increase your awareness of dementia by explaining in depth the behavior and stages of the disease while offering you the tools to manage this journey with understanding and compassion.

Part Two will more specifically equip you to take action in your caregiving as you come to understand the power of acceptance along this journey, how to make adjustments for your loved ones' protection, and how to explore ways to communicate with your loved one from the early stages to the late stages of dementia. You will also gain tools to deal with difficult days and learn what to watch for as behaviors become more challenging with the progression of the disease.

---

[3] "What Is the Life Expectancy for Someone With Dementia?," Age Space, January 19, 2024, https://www.agespace.org/dementia/life-expectancy#:~:text=Type%20of%20Dementia,-The%20type%20of&text=%2D%208%20to%2012%20years.

Finally, Part Three will help you assess your role in your own caregiving. The information will empower you with the keys to prevent burnout and teach you to recognize if it's time to relinquish your role as a caregiver if you're no longer capable of providing what your loved one needs.

You will read of experiences that are on the horizon for you or those that you've already made it through. On the other hand, you might never see some of the experiences you read about here. Either way, my hope is that you'll find value in each chapter.

If you're not feeling a bit more at ease yet, I'm confident you will by the time you finish this book. The stress of the impending changes and challenges you're facing can lead to burnout and guilt, and I don't want you to feel either of those. Burnout and guilt will interrupt your ability to be fully present today and to appropriately grieve when the time comes.

Here is my wish for you: You'll finish this book with tangible tools to help you communicate with your loved one for whom communication is or will soon become a challenge. That communication will make you a better advocate for their needs. You'll also discover ways to find balance, as the many roles you've served in your life before diagnosis still exist and you'll be juggling them. This guide will aid in familial relationships, giving you strategies to help alleviate the conflict that often comes with terminal diagnoses. You'll also learn how to handle the stigma accompanying caregiving and find yourself in a less lonely place than you may have been otherwise. Both your knowledge of dementia and your understanding of yourself will significantly increase. Ultimately, you'll find your pace and learn how to overcome caregiving's expected and unexpected challenges without sacrificing your overall well-being.

I'm happy to lead you on this journey.

I'm Dr. Sam Toroghi, an Internal Medicine specialist in Philadelphia, Pennsylvania. I've taken care of many geriatric patients in different stages of dementia and have served as a consultant for families regarding their home care strategies. My goal is to make serving your loved one, your family, and yourself easier for you. After watching many families struggle to pull together information that would make life after a dementia diagnosis more bearable, I decided to write *The Practical Caregiver Dementia Guide* to offer it all in one place. Knowledge is your most powerful tool. They say when you know better, you do better.

PART ONE
AWARENESS

CHAPTER 1

What Is Dementia?

Before we learn what to expect from the life changes that accompany dementia and how to handle those changes, it's important to understand what dementia is, how the types of dementia vary, and how this disease changes the body and mind. The information in this chapter will provide a thorough framework of how dementia operates that will help you understand each chapter that follows. Of course, parts of this chapter might seem tedious, especially when you read the sections about dementia types that don't apply to your situation. Nevertheless, you may find something interesting and useful in those sections anyway, and you can be confident that the remainder of the book will be applicable to you and your family.

While dementia can be isolating, it is anything but rare. According to the World Health Organization:

- More than 55 million people have dementia worldwide, and each year, there are nearly 10 million new cases.

- Dementia is currently the seventh leading cause of death and one of the major causes of disability and dependency among older people globally.

THE PRACTICAL DEMENTIA CAREGIVER GUIDE

- Women experience higher disability and mortality due to dementia. Women also provide 70% of care hours for people living with the disease.[4]

What exactly is dementia? We know it has to do with severe loss of memory and distinct changes in personality and awareness, but is it a normal part of life? How does a person get it in the first place?

It's important to know that dementia isn't one specific disease. "Dementia" is a catch-all term for the impaired ability to remember, think, or make decisions that interfere with everyday activities. While people often use the terms dementia and Alzheimer's interchangeably, Alzheimer's is actually a type of dementia. In fact, it's the most common type. Knowing its symptoms (what the patient recognizes) and signs (what the caregiver or physician recognizes) will help you move quickly toward diagnosis and treatment. Symptoms of dementia include problems with memory, attention, mood fluctuation, communication, reasoning, judgment, problem-solving, and visual perception beyond what's typical for age-related changes. Signs might include a patient getting lost in a familiar place, using unusual words for familiar objects, forgetting the name of someone close to them, forgetting old memories, or losing the ability to complete routine tasks by themselves.[5]

Since the elderly often display some degree of memory loss, it's logical to wonder whether dementia awaits us all as a normal part of aging. The good news is no, it does not. Normal aging might include loss of muscle tone and weakening bones, stiffening arteries and vessels, changes in memory resulting in the occasional loss of everyday objects, forgetting a word only to remember it later, or forgetting the name of someone you see only on occasion. However, with normal aging, old knowledge and memories remain accessible.[6]

Once you know dementia is not a normal part of aging, the natural next question is, "What causes dementia?" Simply put, dementia stems from

---

[4] World Health Organization: WHO and World Health Organization: WHO, "Dementia," March 15, 2023, https://www.who.int/news-room/fact-sheets/detail/dementia.
[5] World Health Organization: WHO and World Health Organization: WHO, "Dementia."
[6] World Health Organization: WHO and World Health Organization: WHO, "Dementia."

damaged or lost nerve cells and their connections in the brain. The area of the brain that is damaged determines which symptoms manifest, but even still, dementia can have different effects on different people.[7]

Experts categorize the different types of dementia based on what they have in common, like the proteins it produces in the brain or the portion of the brain that's affected. Other diseases and medications can cause reactions that mimic symptoms of dementia, as can insufficient vitamins and minerals. In such cases, treatment can make a difference.[8] Either way, when memory begins to fail, determining the cause is crucial. Physicians can test cognitive abilities, attention span, memory, and problem-solving to see if there's a reason for concern. Additionally, a physical exam, blood test, and brain scan can help determine if there's an underlying cause for the symptoms or if, in fact, dementia is behind these changes.[9]

There are certain risk factors associated with who is more likely to get dementia, including being at least 65 years old, having an immediate family member with dementia, having high blood pressure or high cholesterol, smoking, and having suffered a traumatic brain injury. Race can also play a factor, as older African Americans are twice as likely than whites to develop dementia, while older Hispanics are 1.5 times more likely than their white counterparts to have the disease. But despite the probability based on these risk factors, dementia can strike anyone whose genes are affected.[10]

Genes are specific parts of our DNA that contain information that makes the proteins that build our bodies. We each have over 20,000 genes. Usually, one person has two copies of each gene, one from each parent. A gene variant is when a particular gene differs between different people. If this variant increases the risk of disease, we call this a "risk variant." There are two types of diseases: single-gene diseases and complex or multiple-gene diseases. A

---

[7] World Health Organization: WHO and World Health Organization: WHO, "Dementia."
[8] "Dementia - Symptoms and Causes - Mayo Clinic," Mayo Clinic, February 13, 2024, https://www.mayoclinic.org/diseases-conditions/dementia/symptoms-causes/syc-20352013.
[9] World Health Organization: WHO and World Health Organization: WHO, "Dementia."
[10] World Health Organization: WHO and World Health Organization: WHO, "Dementia."

single-gene disease occurs as a result of changes in only a single gene. This type of disease is rare, when a child inherits such a gene from one or both parents, she will become either a carrier or develops the disease. A complex or multiple-gene disease develops at the intersection of various risk factors, like the person's environment, lifestyle, or multiple gene variants. For these reasons, someone cannot inherit a complex disease the same way they inherit a single-gene disease..[11]

Genetics is often assumed to be the culprit when a disease pattern occurs in a family. However, when family members share a history of complex disease, it's because they likely share other risk factors as well.

Dementia is complex and develops as a result of many combined factors. It is not usually solely caused by genetics. It could result from non-genetic factors, like smoking or diet, with or without inheriting the same gene risk variants as other family members. Since these factors are often shared within the family, you might see a "family history" of dementia. But remember, dementia is not usually a single-gene disease, which makes it much less possible to inherit the disease directly. Even still, a person with high-risk variants might never develop dementia in their lifetime..[12]

The most prevalent risk variant gene discovered for dementia is for Alzheimer's disease. This risk variant is in the apolipoprotein E gene, or the "APOE" gene. There are more than 20 other genetic variants that correlate with Alzheimer's, but they only minimally increase the risk of disease. The APOE gene's variants are APOE2, APOE3, and APOE4. APOE4 carries the most significant risk of dementia development. Genetics determines whether a person gets one, two, or no copies of this gene. The more copies, the higher the risk of Alzheimer's. APOE variants are also risk factors for developing Lewy Body Dementia and Vascular Dementia..[13]

---

[11] "Can Genes Cause Dementia?," Alzheimer's Society, October 8, 2021, https://www.alzheimers.org.uk/about-dementia/risk-factors-and-prevention/can-genes-cause-dementia.
[12] "Can Genes Cause Dementia?"
[13] "Can Genes Cause Dementia?"

The good news is that APOE variants do not guarantee dementia, as they are not a direct cause. Likewise, a person can develop dementia with no copies of APOE4 in their genes.[14]

Rarely, dementia can be caused by a single-gene disease, meaning a parent can pass it on to a child without involvement of other genes or environmental factors. When this happens, the disease has a different personality. It usually develops earlier in life, which is called "Young-onset" Dementia, and there is a tendency for several close family members to develop the same type of dementia. With single-gene dementia, if one parent carries the gene, each child has a 50% chance of inheriting it.[15]

Familial Alzheimer's Disease, or FAD, is a rare form of the disease that's passed through generations. If a parent carries the mutated gene that causes the disease, each child has a 50% chance of inheriting it. They can also develop FAD in their 40s or 50s. Fortunately, this is extremely rare. Genetic testing can identify the presence of the chromosomes that cause this variant of dementia, but it cannot determine when the symptoms will begin. If someone is interested in such testing, first, if possible, they should ensure that a family member had Alzheimer's, not another form of dementia.[16]

While dementia is the catch-all term for a variety of diseases, and often, people wrongly refer to dementia as Alzheimer's, there are several different types of dementia. We will address each of them here.

Obtaining A Diagnosis

When a patient displays cognitive, behavioral, or motor symptoms, dementia should be a consideration. But other disorders, like metabolic disorders, degenerative brain diseases, stroke, or tumors should be ruled out first. To come to a diagnosis, doctors will carry out an assessment that may include a medical interview, blood and urine tests, physical and psychiatric assessments,

---

[14] "Can Genes Cause Dementia?"
[15] World Health Organization: WHO and World Health Organization: WHO, "Dementia."
[16] "Genetics of Dementia," Dementia Australia, n.d., https://www.dementia.org.au/information/genetics-of-dementia.

brain scans, and neuropsychological tests. For some types of dementia, a spinal tap may even be necessary. Family members and caregivers are especially helpful in this part of the process, as they can determine which health problems were pre-existing and which may be dementia symptoms.

Types Of Dementia

Alzheimer's Disease

Medical definition: Alzheimer's is the most common type of dementia. It causes changes in memory, thinking, and behavior by disrupting the brain's neurons and affecting how these neurons communicate.

Prevalence: Alzheimer's becomes more common with age. About one in nine people over the age of 65 has Alzheimer's..[17]

Forms: The two main types of Alzheimer's are sporadic and familial. Sporadic is more common and occurs after the age of 65. Familial is caused by a rare genetic condition and shows up in the patient's 40s or 50s.

Symptoms: The first signs are memory loss and trouble finding the words to express everyday thoughts. Beyond this, Alzheimer's can look like depression. Patients lose interest in activities that used to bring them joy, they become more resistant to change, speech becomes repetitive, and patients get lost in ordinary surroundings.

Causes: In Alzheimer's, the cells and chemicals that control memory, habits, and personality are interrupted by tau proteins (proteins that help stabilize the internal skeletons of nerve cells in the brain) that have become abnormally twisted. The abnormally twisted proteins are called tangles. These tangles disrupt the transport system inside of the cells, and this disruption can cause

---

[17] "Alzheimer's Disease Facts and Figures," Alzheimer's Disease and Dementia, n.d., https://www.alz.org/alzheimers-dementia/facts-figures#:~:text=About%201%20in%209%20people,other%20dementias%20as%20older%20Whites.

nutrients and other essential supplies to fail to move through cells, leading to cell death.

Risk factors: People who don't practice physical and mental exercise, those who smoke, and those with obesity, diabetes, high cholesterol, and high blood pressure are at greater risk of developing Alzheimer's disease.

Vascular Dementia

Medical definition: Vascular dementia, the second most common type, is a form of dementia characterized by damage that results from restricted blood flow in the brain (stroke).

Prevalence: Vascular dementia accounts for about 20% of total patients with dementia.

Forms: The three types of vascular dementia are strategic infarct dementia, multi-infarct dementia, and subcortical vascular dementia. Strategic infarct dementia is categorized by the sudden onset of changes in thinking skills or behavior. It is sometimes caused by one large stroke, depending on its location and size. With this type, if no more strokes occur, the patient can remain stable or improve over time. Multi-infarct dementia is caused by multiple strokes, and as more strokes occur, there is more damage to the brain, accompanied by worsening of symptoms. Subcortical vascular dementia is thought to be the most common type of vascular dementia and is caused by small vessel disease, which affects the small blood vessels deep inside the brain. This type of dementia occurs gradually over time, without sudden episodes of worsening.

Symptoms: Symptoms include difficulty performing tasks that were easy before, getting lost on familiar routes, struggling with language, loss of interest in activities the patient previously enjoyed, misplacing things, and personality changes. These symptoms become more prevalent as the disease progresses and may include changes in sleep patterns, poor judgment, delusions and hallucinations, and withdrawal from social environments. Neurological problems, such as loss of force or sensation in different parts of the body, may also be present due to previous strokes.

Causes: This type of dementia is caused by a major stroke, a series of small strokes, or untreated high blood pressure or diabetes, resulting in vascular disease in small blood vessels in the brain.

Risk factors: Risk factors include high blood pressure, obesity, lack of exercise, tobacco use, and a diet high in saturated fat and salt.

Diagnosis: A series of tests is required to diagnose this particular type of dementia, but ultimately, the diagnosis is made if dementia is present and vascular disease is the most likely cause of the symptoms. If vascular dementia is suspected, a physician may perform a cognitive exam, a complete medical history, blood tests, a neurological exam, a neuropsychological exam, a brain scan, and a carotid ultrasound. A carotid ultrasound checks the two large arteries (carotid arteries) in the neck that supply the brain with oxygen-rich blood. If these arteries are narrower than they should be, there is an increased risk of stroke.

Complications: Complications of vascular dementia include the inability to interact with others or care for oneself, which can eventually result in infections like pneumonia, pressure sores, skin infections, and urinary tract infections.

Lewy Body Dementia

Medical definition: Lewy Body Dementia, or LBD, results from abnormal protein deposits, or "Lewy bodies," in the brain. They affect the brain's chemicals and cause problems with thinking, movement, behavior, and mood.

Prevalence: LBD affects over 1 million people in the United States. Patients usually show symptoms at age 50 or older.

Forms: Lewy Body Dementia covers two closely related conditions. First, there's dementia with Lewy bodies, which affects thinking and memory often at the same time as, or before, problems with movement begin. Then there's Parkinson's Disease Dementia, where memory and thinking problems begin much later, usually a year or more after someone first starts having movement issues, like tremors and stiffness, which are typical of Parkinson's Disease.

Symptoms: Conditions that accompany LBD may include apathy, anxiety, depression, fainting, constipation, urinary incontinence, excessive sleepiness, poor sense of smell, and hallucinations. Patients may experience REM sleep behavioral disorders characterized by acting out their dreams while sleeping so they might yell or hurt their sleep partners. The symptoms a patient experiences depends on which area of the brain is affected and the progression of the disease.[18]

Causes: Scientists don't exactly know what causes LBD, but it is known that the accumulation of Lewy bodies is associated with the disruption of brain neurons that produce two key neurotransmitters: acetylcholine, which is essential for memory and learning, and dopamine, which is crucial for behavior, cognition, movement, motivation, mood, and sleep. Neurotransmitters are chemicals that act as messengers between brain cells.

Risk factors: Age is the most important risk factor for LBD. There is no specific lifestyle factor associated with LBD. However, other diseases, like Parkinson's and sleep disorders, have been linked to a higher risk. Finally, while not a genetic disease, having a family member with LBD may increase the risk.[19]

Complications: Movement problems, sleep disorders, and behavior changes are expected and varied among patients with LBD. Such issues may include muscle rigidity, stooped posture, a change in handwriting, balance problems, difficulty swallowing, a weak voice, sleep disorders (i.e. insomnia and excessive daytime sleepiness), restless leg syndrome, depression, anxiety, agitation, hallucinations, and paranoia. Patients may also experience cardiovascular symptoms, like blood pressure fluctuations and heart rate irregularities, as well

---

[18] "Lewy Body Disease," Dementia Australia, n.d., https://www.dementia.org.au/about-dementia/types-of-dementia/lewy-body-disease.
[19] "What Is Lewy Body Dementia? Causes, Symptoms, and Treatments," National Institute on Aging, n.d., https://www.nia.nih.gov/health/lewy-body-dementia/what-lewy-body-dementia-causes-symptoms-and-treatments.

THE PRACTICAL DEMENTIA CAREGIVER GUIDE

as hormonal and muscular changes, including sweating abnormalities, rigidity, and coordination issues.[20]

Frontotemporal Dementia

Medical definition: Frontotemporal Dementia, or Frontotemporal Disorders (FTD), result from damage to neurons in the frontal and temporal lobes of the brain.[21]

Prevalence: FTD is responsible for less than one in every 20 cases of dementia.[22] Almost a third of patients with FTD have a family history of dementia.[23]

Forms: The three types of FTD are behavioral variant frontotemporal dementia, primary progressive aphasia, and movement disorders.[24]

Symptoms: Symptoms of FTD typically appear between the ages of 40 and 65. However, the disease can affect people younger or older than this.[25] With behavioral variant FTD, there may be changes in behavior, personality, and judgment, but memory will mostly remain intact. Primary progressive aphasia will affect the ability to speak, read, write, and understand what others are saying. Patients may even become mute.[26]

---

[20] "What Is Lewy Body Dementia? Causes, Symptoms, and Treatments."
[21] "What Are Frontotemporal Disorders? Causes, Symptoms, and Treatment," National Institute on Aging, n.d., https://www.nia.nih.gov/health/frontotemporal-disorders/what-are-frontotemporal-disorders-causes-symptoms-and-treatment.
[22] Alzheimer's Research UK, "What Is Frontotemporal Dementia? | Alzheimer's Research UK," January 24, 2024, https://www.alzheimersresearchuk.org/dementia-information/types-of-dementia/frontotemporal-dementia/#:~:text=Frontotemporal%20dementia%2C%20also%20known%20as,younger%20or%20older%20than%20this.
[23] "Frontotemporal Dementia," Dementia Australia, n.d., https://www.dementia.org.au/information/about-dementia/types-of-dementia/frontotemporal-dementia.
[24] "What Are Frontotemporal Disorders? Causes, Symptoms, and Treatment."
[25] "Frontotemporal Dementia."
[26] "What Are Frontotemporal Disorders? Causes, Symptoms, and Treatment."

Causes: The exact cause of FTD remains unknown. Familial FTD is the result of a gene mutation. Those with the disease can have one of several underlying changes in the frontal or temporal lobe or both.[27]

Risk factors: The only known risk factor of FTD is family history. However, most patients have no family history of FTD or any other type of dementia.[28]

Complications: Since there is no cure for FTD and no way to slow down its progression, patients should expect behavior or personality changes, aggression and delusion, a decline in language ability, and issues with movement, such as slowness, stiffness, and balance.[29]

Alcohol-Related Dementia

Medical definition: Drinking too much alcohol over the years can cause Alcohol-Related Dementia (ARD), which presents with memory loss and difficulty in performing daily tasks, like managing finances or cooking.[30]

Prevalence: Population-based studies have reported that one out of every 152 people ages 30-64 years old suffer from this disease.[31]

Symptoms: Symptoms of ARD can vary from person to person. Generally, symptoms include becoming easily distracted; loss of ability to problem-solve, plan, and organize; trouble making judgments; loss of motivation; and insensitivity. Brain scans often show shrinking of some areas of the brain more than others, particularly in the frontal lobe.[32]

---

[27] "Frontotemporal Dementia."
[28] "Frontotemporal Dementia," Dementia Australia, n.d., https://www.dementia.org.au/information/about-dementia/types-of-dementia/frontotemporal-dementia.
[29] "What Are Frontotemporal Disorders? Causes, Symptoms, and Treatment."
[30] "Alcohol-related 'Dementia,'" Alzheimer's Society, n.d., https://www.alzheimers.org.uk/about-dementia/types-dementia/alcohol-related-dementia.
[31] Anniina Palm et al., "Incidence and Mortality of Alcohol-Related Dementia and Wernicke-Korsakoff Syndrome: A Nationwide Register Study," International journal of geriatric psychiatry, August 2022, https://www.ncbi.nlm.nih.gov/pmc/articles/PMC9546078/#:~:text=Population%E2%80%90based%20studies%20have%20reported,beneficiaries%20aged%20%E2%89%A568%20years.&text=A%20Spanish%20study%20reported%20an,%3D%2048)%20of%20ARD%20patients.
[32] "Alcohol-Related 'Dementia,'" n.d.

Causes: Experts are still unclear as to whether alcohol is directly toxic to the brain cells or if brain damage is due to a lack of vitamin B1 (thiamine) that is exacerbated by heavy alcohol use. Problems with nutrition often accompany heavy alcohol use and are contributing factors.

Risk factors: Anyone who drinks excessively over time can develop ARD, but most people do not. Diet and lifestyle may also play a role. It primarily affects men over 45 years old who have a long history of alcohol abuse.[33]

Diagnosis: Making the diagnosis of Alcohol-Related Dementia can be a challenge because the patient will need to abstain from alcohol for weeks to get an accurate measure of their memory. Some experts think an assessment is sufficient as long as the patient is not intoxicated at the time of the evaluation. This assessment may include a paper-based test to check memory and thinking, a physical exam, and a detailed history of the symptoms. There may also be questions about anxiety or depression. A brain scan may be included to rule out a stroke, physical trauma, or a tumor. For a precise diagnosis, the symptoms need to be present even when the patient has stopped drinking, and symptoms should not point to another type of dementia.

Complications: ARD can cause memory problems, loss of ability to understand new information, and loss of knowledge recall, like where patients used to live or places they've been. The patient may have balance issues even when sober, and they may suffer from apathy, depression, or irritability.[34]

Down Syndrome and Alzheimer's Disease

Medical definition: People with Down syndrome have an extra copy of chromosome 21, which carries a gene that produces a protein called amyloid precursor protein, or APP. When APP breaks down, it forms beta-amyloid, or clumping in the plaque that characterizes Alzheimer's. Therefore, compared to the general population, those with Down syndrome have a much higher chance

---

[33] "Alcohol Related Dementia," Dementia Australia, n.d., https://www.dementia.org.au/about-dementia/types-of-dementia/alcohol-related-dementia.
[34] "Alcohol-Related 'Dementia,'" n.d.

of developing Alzheimer's and at a much earlier age. By the age of 40, almost all people with Down syndrome will have brain changes consistent with Alzheimer's Disease. However, not everyone with Down syndrome will develop severe forms of dementia.

Prevalence: Studies show that around 50% of those with Down syndrome will develop Alzheimer's by the age of 60. Symptoms usually appear in the mid-50s.

Symptoms: Symptoms can be hard to recognize, as they may present as further deterioration of existing intellectual difficulties related to Down syndrome. This may include decreased ability to accomplish everyday tasks, loss of short-term memory, increased apathy and inactivity, reduced interest in sociability, confusion, changes in sleep patterns, sadness, anxiety, and restlessness.

HIV Associated Dementia

Medical definition: HIV (Human Immunodeficiency Virus) is a virus that attacks the immune system and can lead to AIDS (Acquired Immune Deficiency Syndrome), the final stage of HIV infection where the immune system is severely damaged. HIV-associated dementia refers to the decline in mental processes as a complication of advanced HIV..[35]

Prevalence: Prevalence of HIV-associated dementia was found to be at 5% of the HIV population..[36]

Forms: HIV-associated dementia (HAD) is the most severe form of HIV-associated neurocognitive disorder, or HAND..[37]

---

[35] "HIV And AIDS Dementia," WebMD, December 31, 2006, https://www.webmd.com/hiv-aids/dementia-hiv-infection.
[36] Yunhe Wang et al., "Global Prevalence and Burden of HIV-associated Neurocognitive Disorder," *Neurology* 95, no. 19 (November 10, 2020), https://doi.org/10.1212/wnl.0000000000010752.
[37] "HIV Associated Dementia," Dementia Australia, n.d., https://www.dementia.org.au/about-dementia/types-of-dementia/aids-related-dementia.

Symptoms: Symptoms may include poor concentration, reduced productivity, difficulty learning new things, changes in behavior and libido, forgetfulness and confusion, aphasia (inability to speak correctly), withdrawal from social settings, and depression.

Causes: Experts don't yet know precisely how HIV damages brain cells. It's possible that viral proteins damage nerve cells directly, or they could infect immune system cells in the brain and spinal cord. Another theory is that HIV causes generalized inflammation, which can lead to memory issues and other aging processes.[38]

Risk factors: While all HIV patients are at risk, other risk factors include diabetes, other infections, older age when HIV is contracted, severely low T-cells (immune cells that are affected by HIV), and inadequate levels of HIV medication (antiretroviral) in the brain.

Complications: Symptoms can progress to sleep disturbances, psychosis, mania, and seizures. If the patient is not using antiretroviral therapy, symptoms can worsen and lead to a vegetative state.[39]

Chronic Traumatic Encephalopathy (CTE) Dementia

Medical definition: Chronic traumatic encephalopathy (CTE) is a type of dementia in which repeated head injuries (concussions or sub-concussions) affect brain function over time at a high enough rate to interfere with the person's normal life.[40]

Prevalence: Recent studies suggest that Chronic Traumatic Encephalopathy (CTE) neuropathologic change might be very uncommon in the general population. The Sydney Brain Bank study reports a neuropathologic change consistent with Chronic Traumatic Encephalopathy (CTE) in less than 1% of

---

[38] "Psychosis: Causes, Symptoms, and Treatment," WebMD, December 27, 2015, https://www.webmd.com/schizophrenia/what-is-psychosis.
[39] "Psychosis: Causes, Symptoms, and Treatment."
[40] "Chronic Traumatic Encephalopathy (CTE) Dementia," Dementia Australia, n.d., https://www.dementia.org.au/about-dementia/types-of-dementia/chronic-traumatic-encephalopathy-dementia.

the examined brains (636 individuals), which included cases with and without neurodegenerative disease.

Symptoms: Not all scientists agree on the symptoms of CTE, but the disease has been associated with memory and thinking problems, confusion, personality changes, and erratic behavior, including aggression..[41]

Risk factors: CTE dementia has been identified in individuals who play sports that involve blows to the head, such as boxing, football, competitive cycling, and others that involve contact or collisions. Otherwise, it can be caused by assault, domestic violence, frequent falls, and explosion or blast trauma. Minor head knocks and concussions can increase the risk; however, a low number of head knocks is unlikely to cause a problem..[42]

Complications: CTE is tricky because signs may not appear until years or decades after the actual injury occurs. Nonetheless, as the disease advances, it can make it hard to pay attention, balance, and control motor skills..[43]

Childhood Dementia

Medical definition: Childhood dementia is a mental disorder that manifests through various symptoms. It cannot be categorized as a specific disease. The medical term for this disease is Neuronal Ceroid Lipofuscinosis, or NCL. There are many types of NCL, and there is no cure for any of them..[44]

Prevalence: Around one in every 2,800 babies globally is born with a condition that causes childhood dementia. This is a relatively low incidence.

Symptoms: Each child's experience with dementia is unique, and symptoms can appear at different ages. Either way, the disease is progressive, and over time, children lose skills and abilities. Symptoms include memory loss,

---

[41] "Chronic Traumatic Encephalopathy (CTE)," Alzheimer's Disease and Dementia, n.d., https://www.alz.org/alzheimers-dementia/what-is-dementia/related_conditions/chronic-traumatic-encephalopathy.
[42] "Chronic Traumatic Encephalopathy (CTE) Dementia."
[43] "Chronic Traumatic Encephalopathy (CTE)."
[44] News-Medical, "Childhood Dementia Signs and Symptoms," September 3, 2018, https://www.news-medical.net/health/Childhood-Dementia-Signs-and-Symptoms.aspx.

confusion, trouble concentrating and communicating, personality changes, severely disturbed sleep, behavioral issues, and emotional issues.

Causes: Childhood dementia results from progressive brain damage and is caused by over 70 rare genetic disorders.

Diagnosis: A physician will reach a diagnosis through either biochemical or genetic testing. These tests may provide a diagnosis or help doctors narrow symptoms down to a group of diseases. Genetic testing then confirms a diagnosis.

Complications: In addition to the symptoms mentioned above, children may also suffer from seizures, lose their vision, hearing, or ability to move, and have problems with several of the body's systems..[45]

Currently, there is no cure for dementia. However, as science evolves, so do better medications that can help control the symptoms and enhance the patient's quality of life. Other therapies, such as talk therapy, oils, herbs, light therapy, and transcutaneous electrical nerve stimulation (TENS), can be helpful to patients. Knowing whether a treatment will benefit a particular patient is hard, as everyone responds differently. Even if a treatment does work, it will take a few weeks for the patients to see some changes. Treatments usually last 6-12 months before symptoms eventually worsen again. It is also unclear whether a medication or treatment will help with the behavioral symptoms of dementia. Still, these therapies can be worth a try.

Knowing which type of dementia your loved one has is key in informing a treatment approach. It's also important to share this information with the patient so they can have knowledge of and agency in their situation. Knowing the causes of dementia will hopefully help to alleviate some of the mystery surrounding the disease and provide tools to help create a roadmap of treatment and expectations.

---

[45] "Childhood Dementia," Dementia Australia, n.d., https://www.dementia.org.au/about-dementia/types-of-dementia/childhood-dementia.

Take Action

Do you know which type of dementia your loved one has? If not, list their symptoms, and compare how your list aligns with the lists we've provided, or go back through the dementia types in this chapter and highlight the symptoms your loved one displays. If a physician has already confirmed your loved one's dementia status, feel free to ask them any questions you might have. If they haven't confirmed a diagnosis, ask them for that confirmation. Find out if any other tests need to be administered and whether medical treatments are available for your loved one.

Understanding the various types of dementia and their characteristics sets the stage for you to understand the importance of early intervention. It will help you empathize with your patient since you now understand what is happening in their mind and body. Next, you'll learn about the stages of dementia and what you can anticipate moving forward.

CHAPTER 2

Understanding the Stages

Tyler had no idea what he was walking into when he stepped on his Aunt Sheila's front porch during Christmas break. But it was clear to me that he was ready to offer any support he could by the way he showed up for his aunt's appointments while he was home.

He and Kendra walked into my office with Sheila, who shuffled in between them. Tyler had the notes open on his phone and sat straight up in his chair, ready to take in all the information he could.

"How is everyone today?" I asked.

Kendra sighed. "It's been ... a day," she replied.

"I'm Tyler, Sheila's nephew," Tyler added. "I just found out about Aunt Sheila's illness when I got home a few days ago. I'm in college, so I'm not here a lot, but I want to help however I can."

I was glad to hear that. Family support is of utmost importance when it comes to dementia care.

"I don't need your help, or anybody else's!" shouted Sheila. "There's nothing wrong with me, and I really wish you'd just let me go home."

I knew not to react. Kendra had learned not to react. Tyler was new to this, but he was excellent at taking cues from the two of us and kept quiet.

"Sheila, I'm glad to see you today. I need to spend a few minutes checking in to see how you are. We won't be here that long, and when we're done, you can head home and get back to your holiday festivities. Sound like a plan?"

Sheila rolled her eyes. "Just hurry up. I got a turkey in the oven."

Kendra pursed her lips. We made eye contact, and she slightly shook her head to let me know there was no turkey in the oven.

"I can see you, Kendra! I wish you people would stop treating me like a child. I'm not a baby. I'm a grown woman. I raised you! And Thomas, I know you're concerned because everybody's making some big deal about me, but I'm the same ol' Aunt Sheila you've always known me to be. I'm just old. Everybody gets old. You'll get old one day and forget things, but it's not a big deal. Can we leave now?"

Kendra took a deep breath and looked at her nephew. "It's okay, *Tyler*," she said, adding extra care to his name. Tyler wiped the tear from his face.

"Everybody here is doing the right thing by coming in for these visits now," I said to reiterate what I'd told Kendra before.

While there are many ways to handle the details of dementia care, the single best plan of action is to seek the help of a physician as soon as dementia symptoms begin to appear.

There are seven stages of dementia, each of which presents its challenges by way of symptoms, risks, and complications. As we explore each one, consider where your loved one may be and whether you're on track for the best possible outcome in your current plan of care.

The Seven Stages of Dementia

Stage 1: No cognitive impairment

No one should ever feel bad about not seeking care in stage one of dementia because the changes in behavior can be almost invisible. There are no obvious signs of mental decline. In fact, the first three stages of dementia, which are referred to as "pre-dementia stages," don't usually present enough change to seek or make a diagnosis, which is why Kendra didn't do so with her sister. Still, know that in this stage, the brain is already changing.

Stage 2: Very mild cognitive decline

Stage 2 symptoms can be difficult to notice because they mirror normal aging behaviors. For this reason, this stage is also called "age-associated memory impairment." Patients might forget information like someone's name or where they've placed their keys. While around 40% of senior citizens have impaired memory linked to age, only about 1% will progress to dementia each year.

When Sheila started losing her keys shortly after entering her house and forgetting the names of people she didn't see regularly, she and Kendra laughed it off and commented about how they were no longer spring chickens. Kendra didn't think her sister's faulty memory was serious, considering she misplaced her own keys all the time, and who could remember the name of any guy they worked with three years ago? The symptoms in Stage 2 are usually still slight enough to miss.

Stage 3: Mild cognitive decline/Mild cognitive impairment

Memory loss becomes more of an issue at this point, but it isn't yet so severe that it impacts daily function. However, according to the National Institute on Aging, it is estimated that 10-20% of people 65 years or older with mild cognitive impairment (MCI) will develop recognizable or diagnosable dementia within a year. If an observer suspects that a loved one's symptoms reflect MCI, it's essential to seek the help of a medical professional. These symptoms include:

- Forgetting to attend events or appointments
- Losing things
- Minor memory loss
- Getting lost while traveling
- Decreased work performance
- Aphasia and verbal repetition
- Challenges when driving
- Trouble concentrating and problem-solving

Sheila and Kendra only saw each other once every week or two, so Kendra missed many of these signs. Since Sheila cherished her independence, she had intentionally kept her distance from her sister once she realized her health was declining. What made Kendra raise an eyebrow was the day she invited her sister to her home, and it took Sheila three times longer than usual to get there. When she called Sheila's cell phone to ask where she was, Sheila didn't answer. Kendra began to worry that Sheila had been in an accident. Just as she was about to call around to track her sister down, Sheila pulled into the driveway.

"What took you so long?" Kendra asked.

"I lost my cell phone and couldn't use the GPS. We're getting to be old ladies, sister!"

That excuse would not have been a concern had they been meeting in an unfamiliar place, but Kendra had lived in the same house for 30 years. She was concerned, so she decided to start keeping a closer eye on her sister.

Stage 4: Moderate cognitive decline

This is the stage in which symptoms of cognitive impairment become more obvious, personality changes become more evident, and most dementia cases begin to be diagnosed. At this stage, a patient can be diagnosed with mild dementia since doctors and caregivers are able to observe language difficulties, reduced problem-solving skills, and other signs that the condition is progressing. These symptoms include:

- Social withdrawal and emotional moodiness
- Lack of responsiveness
- Decline of mental sharpness
- Trouble performing routine tasks
- Forgetting recent events
- Denial of symptoms

The first time I met Sheila and Kendra, Kendra presented me with a list of changes she'd noticed in her sister. In addition to getting lost on what should have been a trip to her home, Sheila had forgotten about Halloween and failed to decorate her home like she'd done every year for decades. She was having difficulty keeping up her garden, and she had transformed from the kind, pragmatic big sister she'd always been to someone who yelled at the slightest inconvenience and denied that anything was wrong. When they came in for their appointment, Sheila was angry that they hadn't arrived at the movie theater like Kendra had promised, but Kendra insisted this was the only way she could get Sheila into my office.

I saw the concern in Kendra's eyes when I told her this stage can last an average of two years. Things were getting difficult, and the difficulties would only progress. I reassured her that while dementia was hard, it wasn't impossible to handle, and I would be there for her every step of the way. I let her know that recruiting the help of family members would be a big help, but carrying the load alone would make the journey exponentially more challenging. This is why I was happy to meet Tyler. Even though he would be away at college most of the time, he took an interest and was willing to help in any way he could.

Stage 5: Moderately severe cognitive decline

Stage 5 is what professionals usually refer to as "mid-stage" dementia. This is when patients struggle with daily activities like getting dressed or bathing. This stage often lasts two to four years; however, each patient progresses at their own rate.

At this point, patients require more support and supervision. They will still remember significant facts about themselves, like their own names and their children's names, but they may forget other family members' names, home addresses, or details about their youth. In addition to pronounced memory loss, patients may display other symptoms like:

- Wandering
- Confusion and forgetfulness
- Disorientation
- Further reduced understanding and problem-solving ability
- Sundown syndrome, defined by patients becoming more irritable, anxious, angry, and irrational at the end of the day.

Sheila had not progressed to this stage yet when she came in for our first meeting, but it wasn't long before she would. Even though Kendra didn't live far away, she wondered if it made more sense for her to move in with Sheila. Once she got a phone call from a family friend that Sheila was wandering aimlessly in the park late at night, Kendra knew it was time, especially as Sheila moved from Stage 5 to Stage 6.

Stage 6: Severe cognitive decline

At this point, patients require a caregiver to help them perform daily activities, such as eating, bathing, and other self-care. Seniors will struggle to regulate sleep, carry on social interactions, or behave appropriately in public. In addition to sleep difficulties, patients may experience:

- Urinary or fecal incontinence
- Aggression and anxiety
- Personality changes, like paranoia or delusions
- Inability to perform daily activities
- Pronounced memory loss
- Failure to recognize loved ones and caregivers

As I consulted further with Kendra, I told her that these behaviors were on the horizon in the coming years. We discussed how it was going to be challenging to watch her sister deteriorate in these ways. I gave her several resources to help her prepare, all of which I'll share in later chapters, including recommendations for support groups. These changes are difficult for the patient and demanding for the caregiver.

Stage 7: Very severe cognitive decline

In the final stage, which is considered late-stage dementia, patients can no longer care for themselves. Generally, they lose all verbal ability, and their movement becomes severely impaired. Other difficulties may include the interruption of bodily functions, like the ability to chew, swallow, or breathe.

As Kendra and I discussed the realities of late-stage dementia, she resolved to make the most of the time they had together rather than mourn the time they expected to lose.

Although there are seven definitive stages of dementia, the progression from one stage to the next is not cut and dry. The symptoms may appear in a different order than what's considered typical, and some stages may even overlap. The amount of care a patient needs at different times can also vary. Some symptoms, especially those linked to behavior, can develop at one stage and reduce in a later one. However, memory loss, language issues, and thinking tend to grow progressively worse over time..[46]

Despite its unpredictable nature, according to the Alzheimer's Society, the tendency is to take two years for early-stage dementia, two to four years for middle-stage dementia, and one to two years for late-stage dementia.[47]

The reason dementia progresses the way it does is because it's caused by different diseases of the brain. In the early stages of all dementia types, only a small part of the brain is damaged. Therefore, a patient has fewer symptoms, which are usually minor. Symptoms vary based on the type of dementia because different types affect different parts of the brain. As dementia progresses, the symptoms tend to become more similar because the affected portions of the brain overlap. The disease spreads until most of the brain suffers damage, which alters all aspects of memory, thinking, language, emotions, behavior, and physicality.

The speed of progression depends on the type of dementia. However, it progresses more quickly if the patient suffers other conditions, such as heart disease, diabetes, or high blood pressure, especially if these conditions aren't managed well.

The patient may experience a sudden change in symptoms; therefore, some patients will need support soon after diagnosis, while others may be able to stay independent for years. Fortunately, there is evidence that people with dementia can adopt certain behaviors and skills to keep their abilities intact longer than they would have otherwise. For example, support and a positive outlook make a big difference. Consuming a healthy diet, avoiding smoking and alcohol, and participating in physical activity can extend healthy days. Other preventative measures, like keeping regular doctor's appointments and

---

[46] Alzheimer's Society, "The Progression and Stages of Dementia," *Factsheet 458LP*, September 2020, https://www.alzheimers.org.uk/sites/default/files/pdf/factsheet_the_progression_of_alzheimers_disease_and_other_dementias.pdf.
[47] Lauren Reed-Guy, "The Stages of Dementia," Healthline, November 27, 2023, https://www.healthline.com/health/dementia/stages#fa-qs.

staying up to date on vaccines, can help the patient avoid new illnesses that could speed up the progression of dementia.

If symptoms suddenly change, it's possible that dementia isn't the reason. If a patient's behavior or mental abilities exhibit a sharp decline over one or two days, this could be a sign of infection or stroke. Under these circumstances, contact a doctor immediately.

Regardless of the type of dementia a patient has, the illness will decrease their life expectancy, which is why dementia is called a "life-limiting condition." While facing mortality is never easy, there are measures the patient and caregivers can take to add quality to the time they have left. This is one reason external support is essential.

Dementia also lowers life expectancy because of the other diseases that can be linked to it. For example, Alzheimer's and Vascular Dementia are closely linked with diabetes and heart disease. Another way dementia reduces life expectancy is by increasing the effects of other severe diseases due to the patient's lowered immunity. Once the patient's immunity weakens, they are likely to develop infections (like pneumonia) or cardiovascular issues (like blood clots in the brain or lungs). Because of these complications, late-stage dementia is usually the shortest.

Additionally, a person with dementia can die at any stage from another condition that has nothing to do with dementia, such as cancer or lung disease. For all these reasons and more, it's hard to say how long a person will live with dementia. There are averages, however.

- **Alzheimer's:** 8-10 years. This number is lower for those diagnosed in their 80s or 90s.

- **Vascular dementia:** around five years. This number is reduced because someone with vascular dementia is likely to die from stroke or heart attack rather than dementia itself.

- **Dementia with Lewy bodies:** around six years.

- **Frontotemporal dementia:** 6-8 years. If a patient also has movement disorders, their dementia tends to progress more quickly..[48]

Early Intervention

Impact of a diagnosis

An early diagnosis is valuable because with a diagnosis comes care and treatment. It also allows the patient to make important decisions about their own care, support, financial decisions, and legal matters. As for support, caregivers can have the information and guidance they need from the start as they navigate the illness and its ever-changing challenges.

Benefits of diagnosis

Dementia can make patients feel like they're losing control, but an early diagnosis can help patients take control of their present situation and the future. A diagnosis helps to avoid other conditions that could be detrimental to their health, which, in turn, helps them preserve their cognition. Additionally, it gives them access to information, resources, support, and medications that could all benefit them tremendously. With early diagnosis comes the opportunity for the patient to share important information with their loved ones while they still can, and there is strong evidence that early diagnosis aids in patients' ability to live independently in their own homes for longer. There are many benefits here, but one that is especially notable is the cost saved on long-term care or hospital stays. Finally, drugs and alternative treatment can be more effective if begun earlier in the life of the illness.

Why it's essential to know the type of dementia

Understanding the type of dementia is crucial because it allows for a tailored approach to treatment and care. Different types of dementia can exhibit unique symptoms and progress at varying rates; thus, specific knowledge enables targeted interventions, more accurate prognostic planning, and access to

---

[48] Alzheimer's Society, "The Progression and Stages of Dementia."

appropriate support and resources. This personalized understanding can significantly improve the quality of life for individuals with dementia and provide their caregivers with the necessary tools and expectations for the journey ahead.

Why people may not want a diagnosis

All of these benefits may seem to make seeking a diagnosis a no-brainer, but the fear of dementia is intense enough to keep people from pursuing the help they need. Fear of losing what they've built professionally and socially is enough to put off testing. However, the benefits of early diagnosis outweigh the fear, as someone may be suffering a treatable condition when they think they're dealing with symptoms of dementia. This fear is not only real for the patient but also for the people in their lives who will be affected by a diagnosis.

Denial may stand in the way of a loved one encouraging someone with the illness to seek help. They may even avoid the subject altogether. However, as dementia progresses, family and friends usually come to accept the condition.

Dementia is life-changing for everyone involved. Therefore, understanding and support are the best tools in the treatment toolbox. I make sure my patients' families know that it's natural to worry, that it's normal to feel out of control, and that once the proper care is situated, everyone will benefit and feel more in control..[49] If there is someone in the patient's support system who is willing to take the lead on pursuing a diagnosis, here are some helpful tips on how to go about it:

- **Ask a friend for help.** Sometimes, people are more apt to listen to friends over family. If there's a friend your loved one respects, ask them if they've noticed the changes in your loved one. If so, ask them if they'd be willing to approach the subject before you or with you..[50]

---

[49] Social Care Institute for Excellence (SCIE), "Dementia - SCIE," SCIE, October 19, 2023, https://www.scie.org.uk/dementia/symptoms/diagnosis/early-diagnosis.asp.
[50] Hdoneux and Hdoneux, "How Do You Convince Your Loved One With Memory Loss to See a Doctor? – Alzheimer's and Dementia Blog – Alzheimer's Association of Northern California and Northern Nevada," *Alzheimer's and Dementia Blog – Alzheimer's Association of Northern California and Northern*

- **Ask your loved one if they'd like you to share information with them.** To see if your loved one is willing to listen to you, ask, "If I noticed that something didn't seem right about your health, would you want me to tell you?" If they say yes, this could be the green light to bring them up to date on the changes you've observed. If they say no, try a different approach.[51] I saw a son use this strategy very effectively with a father who was a military veteran and valued honesty as much as his health. He and his family began noticing the changes at the same time. When someone brought it up, he denied it, saying that he'd been through much worse than a few misplaced items and confusing moments. However, he treasured his son's opinion, which his son knew. So one day his son said, "Dad, you've always told me to be honest with you. If I knew something was wrong but didn't tell you, how would you feel?" This opened the father's ears enough to comply with an assessment and we were able to come to a diagnosis, pinpoint the type of dementia the father had, and begin treatment immediately. The father was happy to learn that his early diagnosis would mean independence that he hadn't expected or considered.

- **Present them with options.** People do not want to feel powerless. Again, dementia can make someone feel like they've completely lost control over their lives. By explaining that there are options for care, such as where they'll live or who will help them, the patient may feel less intimidated by the future and more willing to seek help to extend their quality of life.[52]

- **Turn the focus outward.** By stating that getting help for the patient might alleviate stress on their loved ones, the patient might see the bigger picture and exhibit willingness to seek help in order to help their

---

Nevada - (blog), January 10, 2019, https://www.alzheimersblog.org/2018/04/27/convince-loved-memory-loss-doctor/.
[51] Hdoneux and Hdoneux, "How Do You Convince Your Loved One With Memory Loss to See a Doctor? – Alzheimer's and Dementia Blog – Alzheimers' Association of Northern California and Northern Nevada."
[52] Homage, "How to Convince Your Loved One to Seek Help for Dementia - Homage," May 19, 2022, https://www.homage.sg/resources/how-to-convince-your-loved-one-to-seek-help-for-dementia/.

family and friends.[53] Another patient was requiring more and more assistance from her husband, whom she loved very much. He couldn't retire yet, and she could see the toll that working full-time and caring for her evolving needs was taking on him, but she resisted a diagnosis because she thought it would make things worse. He reached out to me about what to do, and I encouraged him to take this approach. Once he let her know they could pursue assistance if she received a diagnosis and that assistance would help him provide for them more effectively, she got on board with an assessment.

- **Express your concern for the problem without naming it.** The words "dementia" and "Alzheimer's" are frightening words, and words have power. If you can approach the person exhibiting worrisome behaviors by saying, "I've noticed some changes in you that have me concerned," instead of saying, "You've been doing some things that make it seem like you have dementia," the patient might show more willingness to get checked.[54]

Take Action

Consider why your loved one might reject the notion of a diagnosis. Is it because of pride? Is it that they feel they'll lose their position in the family, at work, and in society? Is it because of fear of how the disease will progress? Understanding their motive can help you choose the best way to encourage them to see a doctor. Soliciting the help of other people who are important to them might also be helpful. Make a list of family members and friends who could help convince your loved one to seek a diagnosis.

Knowledge is power. This is especially true when it comes to dementia. Understanding how the disease operates and progresses helps with preparation and decision-making. Sadly, the thought of dementia makes people feel

---

[53] "How to Offer Help to Someone With Dementia Who Doesn't Want It," Alzheimer's Society, n.d., https://www.alzheimers.org.uk/blog/how-offer-help-someone-dementia-who-doesnt-want-it.
[54] Hdoneux and Hdoneux, "How Do You Convince Your Loved One With Memory Loss to See a Doctor? - Alzheimers and Dementia Blog - Alzheimers Association of Northern California and Northern Nevada."

powerless, which can lead to avoidance and denial that can culminate in devastating results. Knowing that early intervention is key, it's important to take action once symptoms start to arise. If the person exhibiting the symptoms refuses help, it's time to get creative. I've found that nothing supersedes compassion when it comes to every aspect of dementia care.

While compassion is key, one of the greatest advantages when dealing with dementia is early intervention. The next chapter will not only stress compassion throughout the diagnosis stage, but also the impacts and benefits of the diagnosis. You'll learn about the symptoms, risks, and complications of dementia along with how to prepare for what's to come.

CHAPTER 3

A Different Perspective

Kendra and Tyler sat in front of the fireplace sipping their cider. The day had been long and busy, so they were glad for the evening's quiet moments. After the rest of the family cleared out, Tyler decided to stay to make sure his aunt was okay.

"Was today hard for you?" asked Tyler.

Kendra smiled. "It sure was," she replied. She took a deep sigh and rocked in her chair.

"How long has Aunt Sheila been doing things like that?"

"Which things? Telling the same stories over and over? Forgetting simple words? For a while. But tripping over the stairs the way she did today? That was new."

"It's hard for me to see her like this. The last time I was home, she seemed fine. A couple of years ago, we ran a 5k together," said Tyler.

"I know. She was so proud. She worked hard to be able to run that race with you."

"How did she get so sick so fast?" asked Tyler.

"I had the same question. Are you okay?" asked Kendra.

Tyler nodded, sipped from his mug, and took a deep breath. "I don't know how you're doing it, but I'll come home more and check on you. I'll help however I can. I just need to absorb all of this."

Tyler's response to what seemed like a rapid change is expected. Dementia can significantly alter the version of a person we've grown accustomed to. To understand how and why someone can change so drastically during the life of dementia, it's essential first to understand some basics about the brain.

Why Do Our Loved Ones Change?

Dementia occurs when the brain is affected by disease. Symptoms vary depending on the section of the brain affected. The brain is an intricate organ, and symptoms appear when the disease interrupts the brain's normal function. Understanding the parts of the brain and their functions helps us understand how dementia occurs when a particular part becomes impaired, so let's look at those parts.

The Cerebral Cortex

The cerebral cortex is a thin layer of cells that covers the outside of the brain. It is responsible for memory, reasoning, decision-making, language, and social skills. It controls actions like walking, talking, and each of the senses. The cerebral cortex is divided into four lobes or regions. These four lobes are:

- Temporal lobes–Located on either side of the brain, these lobes control memory processing, hearing, and language. They store general knowledge. The left lobe helps with language and understanding the meaning of words. The right lobe deals with visual information, such as processing objects and faces. Each lobe has a region called the hippocampus, which processes memories. It stores those memories and makes them available to be found when we want to recall them. Once the hippocampus is damaged, storing new information and memories of events and experiences is difficult. Alzheimer's often begins in or around the hippocampus, which explains why memory loss is one of the first noticeable symptoms.

- Frontal lobes–Right behind the forehead are the frontal lobes, which store and process the information that allows people to make rational decisions and judgments. This is the area most affected in those with Frontotemporal Dementia, causing changes in behavior and personality and difficulty in planning, organizing, and making decisions. This damage also affects the length of attention span, the ability to switch between tasks or juggle interest and motivation, and the ability to filter what is said to others. In some types of dementia, the frontal lobes tend to see damage later in the disease's development.

- Parietal lobes—These lobes are located in the upper section of the back of the brain. The right side helps people understand body positioning and objects in space, such as bringing a fork to the mouth when eating. The left lobe helps people read, write, process numbers, and differentiate between left and right. Damage in these lobes leads to problems with gestures and skilled movements, like getting dressed and brushing your teeth. It can also make reading and writing difficult.

- Occipital lobes–Located at the back of the brain, these lobes deal with visual information, like recognizing colors and shapes, and then pass this information to other parts of the brain. Damage to the occipital lobes eventually occurs in almost all dementia types but not generally in the early stages. When the damage occurs, there can be severe difficulties with visual perception, hallucinations can occur, and eyesight can be damaged.

The brain has right and left hemispheres containing each lobe's right or left side. The lobes do different things, but they work together.

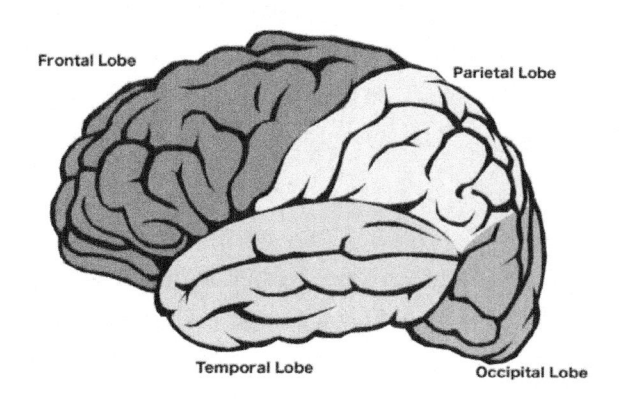

The Sub-Cortex

The sub-cortex allows for fast communication between the different parts of the brain. It refers to any part of the brain below the cerebral cortex containing basal ganglia, the limbic system, the cerebellum, and the brainstem, which are essential for movement, thinking, and emotions.

- **Basal ganglia**—The basal ganglia are a group of structures deep within the sub-cortex primarily involved in controlling movement. Damage to the basal ganglia is common in dementia types associated with movement disorders such as Parkinson's disease dementia, dementia with Lewy bodies, and Huntington's disease dementia. It can result in slow movement, loss of movement, or involuntary movement.

- **Limbic system**—The limbic system is a collection of regions in the brain involved in processing emotions including the amygdala, hippocampus, hypothalamus, and thalamus. Damage to the limbic system is common in most dementias and changes a person's normal feelings or reactions. It can also lead to delusions, like thinking there's a stranger in the house. Additionally, since the hypothalamus (which controls levels of hunger, thirst, body temperature and, to a degree, metabolism) is part of the limbic system, damage can lead to changes in appetite and eating behaviors, like cravings, overeating or obsessions with certain foods. Patients may even try to eat inedible objects. The thalamus sends valuable information to the cerebral cortex and involves consciousness, perception, attention, memory, and movement. The thalamus is also affected in most types of dementia.

- **Cerebellum**—Coordinates movement, balance, posture, and eye function. While new evidence has shown tissue loss in this part of the brain in those with Alzheimer's and Frontotemporal Dementia, few people with these conditions seem to experience cerebellum-related symptoms.

- **Brainstem**—Located at the base of the brain where the spinal cord begins, the brainstem helps control survival functions like heartbeat, breathing rate, blood pressure, sleep cycle, swallowing, and states of consciousness. A region of the brainstem makes dopamine, which is essential for many different brain functions, including movement and feelings of pleasure and reward. Those with Parkinson's Disease Dementia and Lewy Body Dementia often have low dopamine, which makes movement difficult and affects the mood.[55]

---

[55] "Understanding Parts of the Brain," Alzheimer's Society, March 18, 2021, https://www.alzheimers.org.uk/about-dementia/symptoms-and-diagnosis/how-dementia-progresses/parts-brain#content-start.

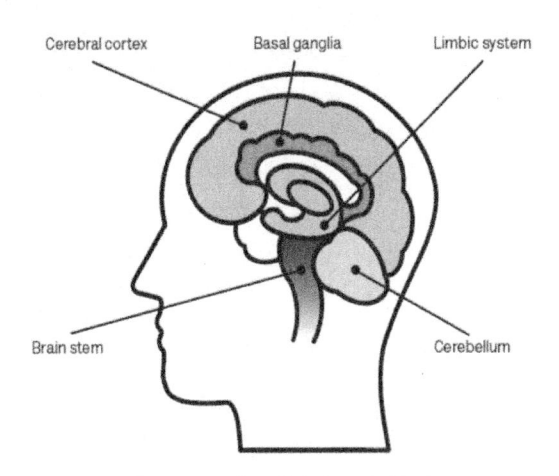

Image credit: Alzheimer's Society

We rely on our brains for everything we do, like the tasks we perform both consciously and subconsciously. As dementia progresses, many of these functions, such as executive function, vision, language, and emotion/behavior, become more difficult.

Executive function is planning, organizing, completing tasks, solving problems, setting goals, and making rational decisions. For this function to occur, the brain must hold information in its working memory long enough to complete the task, like remembering why you've entered a room. This function also involves organizing and planning a sequence of actions, like getting dressed. Also, once executive function is lost, communication becomes difficult, as patients struggle to focus on what they and the other person are saying. It can also become more challenging to hold a conversation while other things are happening in the same vicinity.

Vision, while it may seem simple, requires many different parts of the brain to work together simultaneously. Once the brain is damaged, even if the eyes are in good shape, vision can become a challenge. The occipital lobes gather and process visual data. Then, the temporal lobes associate what the person sees with what they've seen before. Therefore, damage to the temporal lobes can result in recognition problems or the patient seeing things that aren't real.

Damage to the temporal lobes can also mean challenges with language, the process through which we understand and communicate with speech, writing, and gestures. If the temporal lobes are damaged, patients can lose the ability to process what the name of an object is or the use of said object. They may also struggle to find the word they want in conversation. The words they've known the longest are the ones they remember the longest. If they speak multiple languages, they usually revert to the one they learned first.

Communication between the limbic system and frontal lobes controls emotions, so when dementia damages these parts of the brain, patients may exhibit behavior like extreme anxiety, aggression to imagined threats, or laughing when they'd usually cry and vice versa..[56]

If you know which type of dementia your loved one is dealing with, you're probably curious about how the disease will affect their brain and change their behavior. The most common dementia types all start the same: shrinkage of the brain tissue restricts certain parts of the brain, and as the damage spreads, the symptoms become more similar. Let's take a few minutes to explore how the brain behaves in the different dementia types.

Patient Behaviors by Dementia Type

Alzheimer's Disease

With Alzheimer's, the hippocampus and its connecting structures are usually affected first, which makes it hard for patients to form new memories. This is why their speech becomes repetitive. The hippocampus is essential to retrieving recent information, which explains why patients can remember their 10th birthday party but can't remember what they've eaten at an earlier meal on the same day. The amygdala is affected after the hippocampus, causing the patient to recall how they *felt* about something that happened rather than the facts of the event that took place. As the damage spreads and lobes are

---

[56] "Explanation of the Functions of the Brain," Alzheimer's Society, March 18, 2021, https://www.alzheimers.org.uk/about-dementia/symptoms-and-diagnosis/how-dementia-progresses/function-brain#content-start.

affected, the cortex gets thinner, which deletes old memories. After that, the brain shrinks.

Damage to the left hemisphere causes Alzheimer's patients to struggle to find words, and damage to the visual system in the temporal lobes makes it challenging for them to recognize familiar faces and objects. However, since the pathways for vision and hearing are separate, they may still be able to recognize a loved one's voice. If the right lobe becomes damaged, the patient can have difficulty judging distances in three dimensions, so performing such actions as climbing stairs can be challenging. As damage spreads to the frontal lobes, decision-making, planning, or organizing capabilities begin to deteriorate. But all is not lost. Abilities the patient acquired long before, like dancing or playing an instrument, rely on procedural memories that are stored deeply in the brain. Therefore, these skills usually remain the longest.

Sheila experienced many of these changes during the holidays while Tyler visited her home. Once Tyler learned why these things were happening, he felt better prepared to interact with Sheila and had a good idea of what would happen next.

"Atypical" Alzheimer's Disease

In rarer forms of Alzheimer's, in which the hippocampus is not affected first, memory problems are often not the first symptoms to show up. For example, in posterior cortical atrophy, the early damage occurs in the occipital lobes and part of the parietal lobes, which means their vision and spatial awareness will be affected. Take note if the patient exhibits trouble reading, parking a car, or getting dressed.

Vascular Dementia

Since this dementia type is caused by a range of different diseases of the brain's blood supply, the symptoms are more variable than in other types of dementia. This dementia can appear after a major stroke that cuts off the blood supply and destroys a large amount of tissue on one side of the brain. Symptoms may include trouble planning, concentrating, thinking, and recalling memories. It can also cause weakness on one side of the body and problems with vision or speech. Fortunately, with therapy, some recovery may be possible.

Vascular Dementia can also result from several mini strokes over time. Each mini stroke causes a small patch of brain tissue to die, so early symptoms will depend on where in the brain the tissue was lost. For example, if tissue in the frontal lobe is lost, there can be problems with executive function.

Blockage of the small blood vessels in the brain can cause a different type of Vascular Dementia called "Subcortical Vascular Dementia." In this disease, damage to the white matter beneath the cortex will cause slower thinking and challenges with executive function.

Frontotemporal Dementia (FTD)

In all forms of FTD, the frontal and temporal lobes shrink. The different subtypes will reflect different patterns of damage in language and behavior.

In the behavioral variant of FTD, early damage occurs in the frontal lobes. This causes symptoms like isolation, loss of motivation, loss of inhibitions leading to inappropriate comments, and repetition of actions and phrases. In semantic dementia, the front of the left temporal lobe that controls verbal semantic memory is damaged first, making it hard to find the right words for objects or leading to problems with face and object recognition.

I had a patient who had been a long-time school principal. He had the respect of everyone in his small community and was very careful to always present himself with class. One day at a school board meeting, he became loose with his language and told off-color jokes during a presentation. Everyone was taken aback. His assistant knew he had been canceling meetings, which was also out of character for him, and suggested he see a doctor. Although he said he felt fine and chalked his behavior up to exhaustion, he complied with her request. We soon found he had Frontotemporal Dementia. Although the diagnosis was tough to accept, he was relieved to have a reason for his behavior.

Lewy Body Dementia (LBD)

Instead of causing significant shrinkage to the brain like Alzheimer's or FTD, in Lewy Body Dementia proteins deposit into the cerebral cortex, limbic system, and brain stem. Early damage appears in the visual pathways and sometimes the frontal lobes, which could explain why problems with vision and attention are often early symptoms of LBD. Lewy bodies in the brain stem can also be linked to problems with movement such as stiffness, slow mobility, slight shaking, balance, a shuffling walk, less facial expression, trouble with small movements, and sudden muscle twitches, similar to what happens in Parkinson's Disease.[57]

Setting Expectations

Now that you understand what's happening with your loved one, let's focus on you.

While a one-size-fits-all approach to dementia might be helpful, one such solution doesn't exist. Your loved one's diagnosis is unique and therefore, the support you offer them should be what we call "person-centered care." It's important to be sensitive to the patient's needs as an individual, so remember that symptoms may appear in atypical patterns, some patterns may not appear at all, and behavior can change wildly from what you're used to. The key is to focus on your loved one's well-being and approach the diagnosis through the lens of what they still have rather than what they've lost or will soon lose. Furthermore, try to keep their perspective in mind. Their world is changing, too, and the more you understand their coping mechanisms, the better support you can offer.

---

[57] "Dementia Symptoms and Areas of the Brain," Alzheimer's Society, n.d., https://www.alzheimers.org.uk/about-dementia/symptoms-and-diagnosis/how-dementia-progresses/symptoms-brain#content-start.

The patient may cope with changes using:

- Practical strategies, like setting up reminders, preparing important decisions in advance, or establishing a power of attorney
- Social strategies like counting on family for help, spiritual support, or joining new activity groups
- Emotional strategies such as humor, short-term pleasure, and positivity
- Health improvement strategies like exercise, healthy eating, and limited alcohol and smoking

Their response to dementia will depend on various factors including their personality, their previous experiences, their understanding of dementia, their environment, and the social and emotional support they receive. They may use different coping mechanisms at different times. Some people, however, may not acknowledge their dementia diagnosis. Still, some might be aware of the changes in their bodies but choose to chalk it up to age rather than dementia. Their diagnosis may change the way they see themselves, so their support system should do all they can to treat them as an individual instead of defining them by their illness or dwelling on lost abilities. A sense of identity is essential for a person with dementia. Still, a sense of loss can be a significant hurdle in their care.

Behavioral changes can be a source of stress for the patient as well as their family and friends. The patient may become agitated, aggressive, suspicious, or repetitive. This can happen because they have a need they can't communicate. They might be hungry, thirsty, in pain, misunderstood, frustrated, or bored.

Relationships can become strained by a dementia diagnosis. People might separate themselves from their loved one because they're unsure how to act, which isolates the patient. As the disease progresses, they may be unable to support those they previously supported. Caregivers can draw strength from focusing on positive aspects of behavior, like the love and affection the patient continues to exhibit. They can also encourage the patient to participate in community activities, religious services, or hobbies.

As the patient is able to do less, loss of abilities can lead to diminished self-esteem and confidence, fewer social roles and relationships, and the inability to participate in hobbies or everyday activities, like cooking and driving. This loss of independence and communication, and other fundamental changes to their everyday life, can be scary and frustrating.

As a caregiver, be mindful to speak a little more slowly and use simple words and sentences when conversing with your loved one who now finds speech more complicated than it used to be. Pay more attention to body language, like gestures, eye contact, and facial expressions, to better understand what they're trying to say. Try to maintain eye contact, avoid sudden movements, and keep adequate personal space between them and yourself so you don't come off as intimidating. Finally, include them in conversations and avoid speaking on their behalf. They're not invisible and don't want to feel that way. Work on becoming a more active listener and avoid asking too many questions.

Everyone treasures independence, so the patient's support system should strive to let their loved one do things for themselves to maintain their dignity, confidence, and self-esteem. While it's important to let them stay as involved in their own care and decisions as possible, balancing independence with safety concerns is just as essential.

Other ways to help a patient maintain a sense of independence are to do things *with* the patient instead of for them. Focus on their capabilities rather than their "incapabilities." Give them adequate time to complete tasks, break tasks down into more manageable steps, and focus on the process of a task instead of completion.

When patients see they are being supported instead of pitied, relationships have a better chance of remaining strong. A healthy relationship between the patient and the caregiver dramatically contributes to a good quality of life. With this in mind, consider the other ways to nurture the relationship.

Respect what the relationship is in its present iteration rather than what it was in the past. Consider ways to draw attention to the relationship, like looking at photos and retelling stories, creating art and music, and sharing or discovering hobbies. If emotions are strained somehow, spend time apart, when necessary, find a support group and/or sign up for therapy. If you find support you trust, don't be afraid to talk to them about changes in your relationship with your loved one. Sharing is a good release for negative feelings.

Finally, remember that a patient might lose the ability to make certain decisions, but unless they have already shown signs of this, don't assume that they have lost this ability. Keep them involved in their own care and communicate information about their care to them. If they've already shared their wishes with you previously, do all you can to honor those wishes..[58]

I can't stress it enough: when it comes to the most important part of dementia care, nothing tops patience. Your patience with your loved one significantly contributes to their peace of mind and your own. It will give hope when things seem out of control and give you a sense of pride in knowing that you gave your loved one what they needed most when they needed it. When things get overwhelming, don't forget to take a step back and assess the situation. This will help you respond instead of react to things that seem abnormal or overwhelming. It's always good to have a plan but be flexible. Plans sometimes need to change. Learn to grasp what you can and cannot control. Without a clear understanding of these things, you'll get caught in a maze of guilt that serves no one. And finally, be sure to take care of yourself while caring for others. If you never recharge, you'll run out of battery..[59]

---

[58] "Understanding and Supporting a Person With Dementia," Alzheimer's Society, June 27, 2022, https://www.alzheimers.org.uk/get-support/help-dementia-care/understanding-supporting-person-dementia.

[59] Peter R. Abraldes, "Patience When Caring for Someone Living With Dementia - NursePartners, Inc," *NursePartners, Inc* (blog), February 20, 2018, https://www.nursepartners.org/patience-caring-for-someone-living-with-dementia/.

Take Action

Go back through this chapter and pinpoint the type of dementia your loved one has. Underline the symptoms you've noticed in them. Highlight the parts of the brain that have caused these changes, and if there's anything you don't understand or want more information on, write down your questions for your doctor.

After that, highlight 1-3 strategies you can apply to help navigate your relationship with your loved one.

Now that you understand how damage to the brain affects a person with dementia and you know what you can do to help preserve and strengthen the relationship with your loved one as they undergo significant changes, you are probably feeling more prepared to face what comes next. The next chapter will help you understand the intricacies of the diagnosis and how to plan ahead, empowering you to face dementia with grit instead of fear.

PART TWO
ACTION

CHAPTER 4

The First Steps

When I first said the word "dementia," I watched Kendra try to make sense of everything it meant. Sheila wasn't fully aware of what was going on, but she was aware enough to know that something serious had just happened. Kendra halfway paid attention to the dings of her cell phone while trying to process the official name of what she knew to be true. She wondered how long it would be before her sister could no longer remember her name. Her own memories of their childhood and friendship were no longer nostalgic pleasantries; now, they were necessities to fall back on. A tear welled in the corner of her eye, but she quickly soaked it up with the neckline of her T-shirt.

"Okay, so what do we do now?" her voice cracked.

I could have jumped into the names of medications or stressed how important it was not to argue with her sister when she became agitated. Still, I knew the most challenging part of receiving this news was the ability to accept the world they'd just been thrust into.

"We will do several things, but first, I want you to know that you're not alone. I will provide all the resources I can to help you through," I responded.

Dementia is a big word with big implications, and the conversations surrounding it usually center on its struggles. Here, you will find solutions to help you prepare for and navigate the tough times to come. Being a caregiver feels like walking a tightrope over a fiery canyon. Yes, there may be the immediate relief of a diagnosis, as no one enjoys indefinitely chasing the root of a problem. But then comes the fear, frustration, and grief that accompany the diagnosis. What dementia can do to a person has become common knowledge, and it's hard to admit that someone we love will meet such a brutal and often cruel end. Since memories are the proof of our past, the thought that only a few of those memories will exist over time is hard to accept. When it comes to terminal illness, acceptance is often one of the most challenging parts of the process.

Adapting to Change

We know how dementia ends, but it's important to keep in perspective the time you may have with your loved one from now until then. Give everyone involved, including yourself, time to process, and make it clear to your loved one that they are not alone. The comfort of knowing you will be there in the tough times is powerful.

It's normal for a person who's been diagnosed with dementia to feel a sense of loss of their identity. Sheila spent years as an engineer. She'd traveled the world on business and made plenty of time for pleasure. Her home was decorated with pictures and relics of her travels throughout North and South America, Asia, Europe, and Africa. Now she was at risk of forgetting the memories she'd collected. When Kendra thought of all the adventures that had brought her sister joy, she was heartbroken that her sister wouldn't be able to hold on to those memories. And Sheila refused to believe things were changing for her, which is a normal reaction. A part of your role as a caretaker is to remind the patient that there is still a life to live. You can help them get beyond the all-consuming feelings of loss by assisting them in engaging in meaningful activities, which might mean continuing to do things they already love or finding something new that might give them a sense of purpose.

The best course of action is to ask the patient how they would like to spend their days. By learning what brings them purpose, you give them a sense of ownership in their own decisions, immediately making them feel less at the mercy of the disease. Additionally, you can decide on activities to do together, find opportunities in the community that speak to their interests, try something new altogether, or encourage them to connect with others in their position to see how they've chosen to participate in their own lives.[60]

While seeking out a community for your loved one, remember to assemble one for yourself. Reach out to your support system. If you don't have one, get one. You're going to need it. Make sure to keep this circle tight with empathy. Dementia is a stressful and dynamic human experience, and to get through it, you need to be surrounded by people who will provide encouragement and practical advice. It is easy to lose yourself in the caregiver role. In fact, it's common for caregivers to become sick while looking after someone else without even realizing it. Do your best to maintain a sense of self while doing this work and remember that looking after your loved one is only a part of who you are. Janet, my patient David's wife, is a prime example of how to do this.

Janet and David had just celebrated their 50th anniversary when they learned David was sick. David had always promised he'd never become one of "those men" who forgot the important dates in their marriage. To prove it, he always wished Janet a happy anniversary before she could say it to him. So, when 9:00 a.m. approached on the morning of their 50th anniversary, and he still hadn't mentioned the milestone, Janet knew something was wrong.

Janet had watched David's mother as his father had gone through this. Upon David's diagnosis, Janet resolved to handle the situation with the same grace as her mother-in-law had. That meant documenting the time she and David had left as well as protecting the time she was able to spend doing the things that made her happy, like going to Sunday brunch with her friends and exploring the new displays at the art gallery every other Friday. These moments of respite are essential, as dementia can often become emotionally exhausting.

One symptom of dementia is a shift in emotional responses. The patient might have less control over their feelings, causing them to overreact or become

---

[60] "Accepting the Diagnosis," Alzheimer's Disease and Dementia, n.d., https://www.alz.org/help-support/caregiving/stages-behaviors/accepting_the_diagnosis.

irritable. They might become distant, disinterested, or difficult. It's important to remember that these changes aren't personal; much of it is because of the damage to the brain. The key is to look beyond surface behaviors and try to understand where these feelings are coming from. It's possible that the patient is reacting to what they perceive as unmet physical or emotional needs. For example, they may feel out of control of their own lives, like they can't trust their judgment, or they may feel socially demoted because they can't do the things they used to do. It could be that they feel overwhelmed by the effects of the disease on their health, finances, employment, and relationships.[61]

Leonard had always been a distant father. His perspective on life continued into his time as a grandfather. Although he lived close to his family, he didn't see the need to spend much time with them. He would show up for the big events of their lives, but as far as he was concerned, everyday life was for them, and his everyday life was for himself. People knew something was wrong when he started dressing shabbily and wandering in the street instead of walking with purpose as he'd always done on his daily strolls. Still, the most notable change came after he'd been admitted to a long-term care facility. Whenever his family would visit him, he'd burst into tears and ruminate, "You're everything to me! I want you to stay here forever because you're everything to me!" His children and grandchildren didn't know how to react, but they wished he'd have been just as vulnerable during all the years he'd missed with them.

Dementia is a lot to take in, so it's important to allow the people involved the time to come to a place of acceptance of what is happening. According to corewoodcare.com, actions that help come to acceptance include:

- Allowing yourself the time to adjust
- Learning about the disease

---

[61] "Redirect Notice," n.d., https://www.google.com/url?q=https://www.alzheimers.org.uk/get-support/help-dementia-care/understanding-supporting-person-dementia-psychological-emotional-impact%23content-start&sa=D&source=docs&ust=1700597893263681&usg=AOvVaw0v_StyNEDGstR00WZi0yAq.

- Resting
- Exercising
- Setting up routines and expectations
- Seeking counseling
- Hiring a caregiver [62]

Consider that your loved one might not understand or accept the fact that they are ill. If they go through a period of denial, you must be patient with them. In the meantime, you can do helpful things like assess the safety of their home and their ability to drive. [63]

Whether immediately or after denial has worn off, the patient must also come to grips with this new reality. In the early stages after diagnosis, as you digest the significant changes to come, give the patient time to do the same. It's perfectly normal and acceptable for them to feel upset about how they are changing. While they are considering the changes at hand, emphasize the roles and responsibilities in their life that still make them who they are, like being a grandparent, parent, sister, or brother. They might also find it beneficial to speak with a professional—like a counselor, therapist, or clergyperson—about the diagnosis. [64]

Planning and Important Decisions to Consider

Dementia affects the patient's memory before a diagnosis is reached, hence the need to seek a diagnosis in the first place. On average, people live ten years after diagnosis. This slow fade of memory loss is called "the long goodbye."

---

[62] Tim, Corewood Care, and Tim, "How to Handle Dementia in Loved Ones - Corewood Care," Corewood Care - Home Care & Care Management, May 22, 2023, https://corewoodcare.com/handling-dementia-in-loved-ones/.

[63] Angelike Gaunt, "What to Do When a Parent Is Diagnosed With Dementia: 10 Steps to Help You Move Forward," January 2, 2024, https://www.aplaceformom.com/caregiver-resources/articles/after-dementia-diagnosis.

[64] Agency for Integrated Care, "Help Loved One Accept Dementia Diagnosis - Agency for Integrated Care," August 12, 2023, https://www.aic.sg/caregiving/help-loved-one-accept-dementia-diagnosis/.

Because the patient's memory can fade at unpredictable levels, there are actions the caregiver should take as early as possible to alleviate as much stress as possible both now and later.

While the patient can still make decisions, have a conversation about the illness and their end-of-life care, then make it top priority to honor those wishes. Learn about the disease together, and together, if your loved one is able to contribute, hash out the details of their treatment.

Sheila wasn't interested in discussing the details of her diagnosis outright. Still, she relented long enough to share important information with Kendra concerning plans she'd already made for herself in case anything ever happened to her.

"I don't care what any doctor or tests have to say," she said. "I don't have dementia. That doesn't run in our family. But I am getting older, and I figure now is as good a time as any to let you know that I've already worked things out in case I do get sick or just fall out and die one day. If you look in the top drawer of my bureau, it's got all the information you need. Insurance, bank account numbers—I even planned my funeral. I've set money aside for anything expensive. I know how much it costs to be sick. Use it if you ever need it."

Although Kendra was reeling with the news of the diagnosis, planning what to do in case of a variety of scenarios, and sharing the news with people who needed to know about Sheila's condition, she was relieved that her sister had taken it upon herself to plan for her later years. Sheila was secretive and hyper-independent, so it comforted Kendra that her sister trusted her to take care of her at the end of her life, a responsibility Kendra took seriously.

Loss of independence is a significant loss. If your loved one has already made plans for themselves in case of sickness, it's an act of respect to ensure those plans won't be in vain. If they haven't already made plans, doing this together will give them a boost of independence during this vulnerable time. Additionally, maintaining the things in life that bring them joy is crucial in helping them accept reality. If they played games before, they still like games now, so continue to play with them as long as they are able. Provide foods they enjoy, and if those foods aren't healthy, simply give less of them and replace them with more nutritious foods that are also sweet or savory, whatever their preference. The life of a dementia patient doesn't need to become a prison.[65]

It's important to share diagnosis news with the patient's family and friends. This way, everyone can make the necessary adjustments to the expectations of the patient's role in their lives and their own interactions. While sharing the news can be a difficult conversation to have, it is necessary, and the sooner, the better. While each situation may look different, there are some guidelines to keep in mind:

- Get the consent of the patient before sharing their diagnosis.
- Be factual about the symptoms and how the disease might progress. Involve the patient in the process if you can.
- If you need support as the caregiver, let people know. Be direct and specific about your needs.
- Focus on the here and now instead of what's to come.
- Involve family and friends in familiar activities.[66]
- Share the news in a quiet, relaxed environment.
- Bring information or notes from reliable sources to share with the family.

---

[65] "How to Help a Loved One With Alzheimer's or Dementia," Cedars-Sinai, n.d., https://www.cedars-sinai.org/blog/how-to-help-a-loved-one-with-alzheimers-or-dementia.html.
[66] "What Is Dementia and Its Impact on Daily Life as a Carer," n.d., https://www.carersfirst.org.uk/caring-for-someone-with/dementia-how-to-tell-family-and-friends/.

- Expect different reactions and give people space to express how they feel.[67]

Even though Sheila wasn't the picture of compliance concerning her diagnosis, Kendra took the opportunity to share as much information as possible with Tyler while he was home from college on winter break. I had given Kendra pamphlets and websites for reference, and she passed this information on to Tyler. Tyler insisted Kendra keep him updated on any changes, and Kendra agreed. Together, they made a list of family members and friends who might have been able to help in different ways. Sheila had been on her own for most of her life and fortunately, she was organized. She had also done very well planning for her later years, which turned out to be helpful for Kendra, Tyler, and anyone else who would lean in to help. Physical assistance, emotional support, and financial resources are tremendous, considering the challenges a dementia diagnosis can pose to the patient and their family.

According to AJMC, the cost of dementia treatment is projected to increase from $321 billion in 2022 to over $1 trillion by 2050. Today, Medicare and Medicaid account for about two-thirds of these costs, with the remaining costs being absorbed by family members, private insurance, health maintenance or managed care organizations, and uncompensated care. Additionally, caregivers of dementia patients bore nearly twice the average out-of-pocket costs than those caring for patients without dementia.[68]

As previously mentioned, family caregivers are vulnerable to the health consequences of the chronic stressors associated with dementia caregiving. Many caregivers are socioeconomically and medically vulnerable. Women represent 58% of all dementia caregivers, and 42% of caregivers have a

---

[67] Lifted Team, "How Do I Tell Family and Friends About a Dementia Diagnosis? - Lifted," Lifted, March 30, 2023, https://www.liftedcare.com/news/how-do-i-tell-family-and-friends-about-a-dementia-diagnosis/.
[68] Anita Pothen Skaria PharmD, "The Economic and Societal Burden of Alzheimer Disease: Managed Care Considerations," *AJMC*, November 8, 2 022, https://www.ajmc.com/view/the-economic-and-societal-burden-of-alzheimer-disease-managed-care-considerations.

household income of $50,000 or less. Caregiving means disruptions in work schedules and sometimes, the need to leave the workforce altogether.[69]

According to a University of Michigan Institute for Healthcare Policy & Innovation study, by the end of two years, households with dementia patients saw their average wealth drop from $79,000 to $58,000, and their out-of-pocket costs doubled to around $8,000. Their peers saw neither of these impacts.[70]

Additionally, "by the end of eight years, people with dementia had spent twice as much as their peers out of their own pockets for health expenses and had seen their wealth drop to an average of $30,500 while their peers saw no significant drop."[71]

With such a significant financial impact, planning as much as possible is necessary. Nevertheless, finances aren't the only element of planning that needs attention. An array of decisions needs to be made, and they need to be made sooner rather than later.

Healthcare planning becomes immediately crucial in the face of a diagnosis. It helps to alleviate the caregiver's responsibility by setting in writing a living will, which gives doctors information about the patient's desire for treatment, and power of attorney, which enables someone to make medical decisions for the patient in case they're unable to do so. These medical decisions can be the difference between continued treatment or comfort care measures. In its late stages, dementia can make it hard to swallow, which can then allow food or liquid into the lungs and cause pneumonia. If that happens, there may be a need for a feeding tube to provide nutrition, a ventilator to help the patient breathe, or antibiotics to fight lung infection. However, everyone might not want to take these measures. This is why it's vital to discuss decisions such as:

---

[69] "Dementia's Financial & Family Impact: New Study Shows Outsize Toll," Institute for Healthcare Policy & Innovation, n.d., https://ihpi.umich.edu/news/dementias-financial-family-impact-new-study-shows-outsize-toll.
[70] "Dementia's Financial & Family Impact: New Study Shows Outsize Toll."
[71] "Dementia's Financial & Family Impact: New Study Shows Outsize Toll."

- **Do not intubate order (DNI)**—a directive that informs medical staff that you do not want to be put on a breathing machine.

- **Do not resuscitate order (DNR)**—a directive that lets medical staff know you do not want CPR or life support in case breathing or heartbeat stops.

- **Organ and tissue donation**, which allows for healthy organs to be transplanted into someone who needs them

- **Brain donation for scientific research**, which allows scientists to study the brain for dementia treatment and prevention.[72]

Financial planning involves a will, which clarifies how assets will be distributed after death; a durable power of attorney for finances, which names someone to make financial decisions in case the patient is unable; and a living trust, which names a "trustee" to hold funds and property when the patient can no longer manage their own affairs.[73]

It's also important to take inventory of all the patient's assets and debts and identify all family members who need to know about the patient's financial situation or who can provide support. Once you've identified the cost of care, it's important to explore avenues that could offer financial assistance, such as government benefits, long-term insurance policies, and veterans benefits, if applicable. If the economic situation is complicated, a financial planner can be an excellent resource.[74]

One patient, Leonard, had served in the U.S. Army for years. He was living alone, and he was in pretty bad shape when he got to me for an assessment. We contacted his son, Derrick, who could visit and offer help for a few days but couldn't care for his father long-term. After going through his father's

---

[72] "Planning After a Dementia Diagnosis | Alzheimers.gov," n.d., https://www.alzheimers.gov/life-with-dementia/planning-for-future#health-care-planning.
[73] "Planning After a Dementia Diagnosis | Alzheimers.gov," n.d., https://www.alzheimers.gov/life-with-dementia/planning-for-future.
[74] "Financial Planning," Alzheimer's Disease and Dementia, n.d., https://www.alz.org/help-support/i-have-alz/plan-for-your-future/financial_planning.

paperwork and making several phone calls, Derrick learned his father was eligible for long-term care at the veteran's home the next town over. This was of huge financial help and provided the full-time care Leonard needed.

Long-term care planning includes wishes for where the patient will live as they age and identifies resources and costs available in the community. Because dementia can cause behaviors like wandering and aggression, it makes sense for loved ones to start considering long-term care planning as soon as a diagnosis is made. This care can happen in the home or a long-term care facility. Consider where the patient will be able to get the best support, the cost of services available in their community, and how far you may be from needing to move them into this phase of care..[75] Find out if Medicare or Medicaid coverage is available for your loved one, and if your state has a department of aging that provides assistance. If you have any questions, call the Alzheimer's Association Helpline at 800-272-3900. Someone is available 24/7 to answer your questions..[76]

When Sheila and Kendra were young, they were partially responsible for caring for their grandfather who had come to live with them when he fell ill. Sheila remembers this as an unpleasant experience that she didn't want anyone to have on account of her. So, in the notes in her top drawer, she'd included pamphlets for long-term care facilities she wanted Kendra to consider if the time ever came when she might need it.

There is no cure for dementia, therefore, **end-of-life planning** is a complex task that needs your attention. This planning includes early discussions with family members about where and how the patient wants to die, what they want their funeral to be like, and the location of their paperwork and essential documents. If conversations concerning a will, advance directives, a DNI, a

---

[75] "Planning After a Dementia Diagnosis | Alzheimers.gov," n.d., https://www.alzheimers.gov/life-with-dementia/planning-for-future#long-term-care-planning.
[76] Brian P. Dunleavy, "Caregiving for Dementia: 8 Key Steps for Care Planning," EverydayHealth.com, November 21, 2022, https://www.everydayhealth.com/dementia/caregiving-for-dementia-key-steps-for-care-planning/.

THE PRACTICAL DEMENTIA CAREGIVER GUIDE

DNR, and other directives have already taken place, the end-of-life planning stage will be exponentially more manageable.[77]

Take Action

Take a deep breath. I know this is a lot to consider. The diagnosis is jarring enough and all of this information about what to do next, while helpful, can quickly become overwhelming. Let's take a moment to break these considerations into tasks to make things more manageable. Answer the following questions:

1. What was your loved one's reaction to their dementia diagnosis? What was your reaction?

2. Who is in your support system, and what role does each person serve?

3. Have you shared the diagnosis with other family members and friends? How did you go about it? If you haven't done so yet, how will you do it? Do you need help with the plan?

4. Do you have a financial plan in place as the disease progresses? If not, what resources could benefit you?

5. Are you aware of your loved one's insurance benefits?

6. Is there a living will, power of attorney, DNI, or DNR in place? What about organ donor paperwork? Are there any other orders to consider that you should ask a care professional about?

7. Have you and your loved one considered the best option for long-term care when the time comes? If so, what is the plan?

8. Have you had conversations about what end-of-life will look like when the time comes? What are those plans?

---

[77] Dunleavy, "Caregiving for Dementia: 8 Key Steps for Care Planning."

Dementia provides a membership to a club no one wants to be in, but once you're there, the more helpful resources you have, the better. When you know what to expect and how to prepare for long-term care and end-of-life decisions, the experience is much more bearable. By gathering this information as soon as possible, you'll shorten your to-do list and give your loved one and yourself more time for the adjustment period that will come next.

The adjustment period is critical to creating an environment that will ensure the patient's safety. As dementia progresses, the world will start to feel less safe for your loved one. Even familiar places, like their home, can pose new dangers you haven't considered before. The next chapter will inform you of obvious and hidden hazards that could make a big difference in your loved one's health and safety.

Share Your Heart, Share Your Review

Empower Caregivers Together

"The greatest good you can do for another is not just to share your riches, but to reveal to them their own."
- Benjamin Disraeli.

Helping others without expecting anything in return is a path to true happiness and fulfillment. People who give selflessly often lead more joyful and rewarding lives. As a caregiver, you are already dedicating a significant amount of your time and energy to caring for a loved one. Imagine if you could extend that dedication and selflessness to others in need.

Would you be willing to help someone you've never met without seeking recognition for your actions?

You might wonder who this person is. They are a lot like you once were: kind, eager to provide the best care for their loved one, a little unsure and looking for guidance on how to do it effectively, yet uncertain about where to begin.

Our mission is crystal clear: to make the journey of dementia caregiving understandable and manageable for everyone involved. Every action we take serves this goal. Reaching out to as many people as possible is the only way to fulfill this mission effectively.

Here's where you play a crucial role. The reality is people do judge a book by its cover—and its reviews. So, on behalf of countless caregivers out there in need:

Please consider leaving a review for this book.

It's a simple act that doesn't cost a dime and takes barely a minute of your time. Yet, it could profoundly affect another caregiver's life. Your thoughtful review could be the beacon of hope for...

- another caregiver to provide the best possible care for their loved one.
- another dementia patient to receive the love and care they deserve.
- another family member to avoid the dreaded caregiver burnout.
- another household to discover new ways to thrive amidst challenges.

Achieving that heartwarming feeling and making a tangible difference is easy—just leave a review.

Scan the QR code below to leave your review on Amazon.

https://www.amazon.com/review/review-your-purchases/?asin=B0D2JMJSSV

If the thought of aiding a caregiver you may never meet warms your heart, then you're exactly the kind of person we adore. Welcome to the family.

A heartfelt thank you for your generosity. Now, let's dive back into our guide.

Your devoted supporter, Sam Toroghi, MD

CHAPTER 5

Adjusting Period

After Tyler returned to his university after the break, Kendra was left to care for Sheila alone. It seemed that Sheila's condition got worse immediately. Perhaps it did, or maybe it just felt like it did because Kendra was left as the sole caregiver. Either way, her stress multiplied.

Sheila wanted to know where "Thomas" had gone, and she became angry when he didn't show back up. On top of that, she'd developed a temper with her sister. Kendra felt like she couldn't do anything right. Sheila started yelling at anyone who came to the door—the mailman, the food delivery person, children selling items for fundraisers, or even the neighbor's dog who occasionally wandered onto the porch. Kendra felt bad for her sister, and she felt bad for herself. At first, she would return Sheila's insults, but she'd feel immediately guilty because she knew this wasn't the same Sheila she'd always known. She longed for the days before dementia and hoped that this new life wouldn't go on for decades, which only made her feel guilty for wanting the whole thing to be over. When she contacted me, I told her the way she was feeling was normal. Dementia often feels impossible, and it takes constant adjustments to get through each day. In addition to understanding, I offered her some coping mechanisms.

The Stresses of Caregiving

Over the years, I've watched my patients' loved ones, like Kendra, suffer more than they need to. They're frustrated with the challenges that come with dementia, and on top of that, they feel guilty for being frustrated. Frustration is to be expected. You're human and dementia is difficult.

Warning Signs of Frustration

According to caregiver.org, signs of frustration include:

- Shortness of breath
- A knot in the throat
- Stomach cramps
- Chest pains
- Headache
- Compulsive eating
- Excessive alcohol consumption
- Increased smoking
- Lack of patience
- Desire to strike out

When dementia transforms your loved one into a new person, you are justified in your feelings. However, keeping your emotions in check is vital so you handle the patient with care instead of anger.

Managing Effectively

Frustration comes from a place of helplessness; therefore, it's essential to recognize what you can and cannot control. There will be many situations along this journey that make you feel powerless. Fortunately, the one thing you can control is your response to these feelings. Learn to recognize triggers and warning signs, practice deep breathing and mindfulness, change your way of thinking about the situation, practice assertive communication techniques, and last but not least, don't be afraid to ask for help.

Calming Down Physically

You're no longer at the mercy of your feelings when you notice the signs of frustration. Instead, you can implement strategies to calm yourself down. If possible, separate yourself from the situation to avoid doing or saying something you might regret later. If you think you might offend someone by leaving the room, say you need to go to the bathroom or are getting some fresh air. Try a few different calming methods to find what works for you, like deep breathing, taking a walk, meditating, praying, listening to music, or taking a shower or bath. Additionally, practicing relaxation techniques regularly like deep breathing or meditation can help you remain proactive in frustrating circumstances.

Modifying Your Thoughts

They say it's not what happens to us that makes a difference. Instead, it's how we feel about what happens to us. And what determines how we feel? Our thoughts. It is indeed a natural human response to feel an array of emotions under challenging circumstances. Still, if we don't keep those thoughts in check, it's easy to let negativity rule our thinking. Dealing with dementia will make you feel out of control in many ways. Fortunately, one thing you can control is your thought pattern. Let's take a look at negative thought patterns that can make a challenging situation feel downright unbearable. After that, we'll counter negative thought patterns with helpful, adaptive responses.

Overgeneralization

Overgeneralization is taking a frustrating instance and applying the feelings about that thing to everything. For example, if you're cooking dinner for your loved one and the spaghetti falls onto the floor, overgeneralizing is thinking,

"If it's not one thing, it's another. Why can't everything just go right for once?" An adaptive response to the situation would be, "Hey, it happens. Compared to everything that went right today, this isn't even noteworthy. Besides, I have another pack of spaghetti right here."

Discounting the positive

Instead of giving credit where it's due, you minimize actions that deserve attention. For example, if someone commends you for the care you give to your sick loved one, you respond with, "It's not that big a deal. People do this every day." An adaptive response to the situation could be, "Thank you. It's a challenge that I do my best to handle with strength and attention. I appreciate that you noticed."

Jumping to conclusions

This involves assuming you know the motives or reasons behind someone's actions. Jumping to conclusions can take two forms. The first is mindreading, in which we assume others think negatively about us. For example, if we wave at someone in public and they don't wave back, we might assume they're angry with us or that we've somehow offended them. An adaptive response would be to assume they just didn't see us or to reach out to them to make sure they're doing okay. Another form of jumping to conclusions is fortune-telling, which is predicting a negative outcome in the future. For example, you may not be interested in joining a support group because "Talking about it won't help anything, anyway." An adaptive response would be, "It might help to get some things off my chest. At the very least, I'll be around people who understand."

"Should" statements

The connotation of the word "should" suggests that you aren't doing something you are supposed to be doing, and the thing you are neglecting conflicts with what you really want to do. For example, you might say, "I shouldn't go out to eat today. What if someone needs me while I'm out?" This thinking can leave you feeling guilty or depressed. An adaptive response could be, "It's okay for me to take an hour or two for myself today. I'll ask someone to look after things while I'm gone."

Labeling

Labeling is identifying yourself or someone else by one action. For example, if you order take-out instead of cooking, you might think, "I'm lazy and irresponsible with money." An adaptive response could be, "This is the only day I've ordered take-out this week. It was a hard week, and I won't feel bad about taking a break from cooking."

Personalizing

Personalizing means taking responsibility for circumstances beyond your control, like blaming yourself for a loved one's health decline. An adaptive response would be, "I've done everything I could to help, but the attention my loved one needs is now beyond what's in my expertise to provide for them."

It's easy to fall into negative thought patterns, especially when stress is high. Still, it's worth it to take an extra step to redo those thought patterns and follow more positive ones. When something happens, or you notice yourself thinking negatively, take a pause, notice the negative thought, and replace it with a more adaptive idea.

Communicating Assertively

One way to reduce confusion and frustration is through assertive communication. This is different from passive or aggressive communication. Passive communication does not explicitly express your needs and desires, and aggressive communication can be disrespectful and incomplete, which makes those you're trying to communicate with defensive. However, assertive communication focuses on your desires and the needs of others, opening the door to respectful discussion about pressing issues. When speaking assertively, respect your own thoughts and feelings, express your thoughts and feelings without shaming or humiliating anyone else, use "I" statements instead of "you" statements, and avoid "should statements." Here are some examples:

"You" statement	"I" statement
You are so disrespectful when you talk to me.	When you speak to me like that, I feel like my hard work goes unnoticed.
You don't care about anyone but yourself.	When you don't do what we agreed to, I feel like our plan isn't important to you.
You're always late, and Mom has missed important appointments because of you.	When you're late, it comes across that this isn't a priority. Is there anything I can do to help these appointments align with your schedule more consistently?

"Should" statement	Alternative
I should have known better than to say that.	Next time, I will be more in tune with the possible effects of my words.
I shouldn't take a day to myself. What if something happens?	I can only control what I can control. I'm a better caregiver when I have time to myself.
Somebody ought to help me. I can't do this alone!	I will be more open to asking for and receiving help so I'm not always exhausted.

The Critical Step: Asking for Help

Caregiving is a huge responsibility. It is the work of a team, not an individual. Asking for help is not an option; it's a necessity. People understand this, so don't feel like you're imposing when you ask someone else to help. Discuss the situation and your needs with family and friends to see who might be willing to step in and take on some of the responsibility.

Kendra knew she couldn't handle the long periods of caring for her sister alone between Tyler's visits, so she decided to reach out to Sheila's friend Meredith, someone she'd worked with for years. Kendra was nervous to ask for help. She knew Meredith had their own life and didn't want to impose. After a discussion with my nurse and me, she called Meredith, explained Sheila's situation, and asked her if she could come over once or twice a week to help with the daily schedule and give Kendra a break. Meredith travels often, so she couldn't commit to every week, but she promised to help whenever she was in town.

If someone agrees or offers to help, don't be afraid to accept it. There is nothing noble in taking on the responsibilities of a caregiver alone. Don't wait until you're in a bind to reach out. Be assertive about what you need and when you need it and remember, people like to help. It makes them feel useful and part of the solution, and it's an expression of love for them as much as it is for you. You can ask others to visit with your loved one and chat, prepare or order food, or help with yard work or laundry. You may also ask those who are willing to pitch in to give the patient a ride to appointments or stay with them for a few hours while you take time away from caregiving.

As for yourself, boundaries are vital. As a caregiver, you're pulled in many different directions. Learn when to say no and permit yourself to do so without feeling guilty. You're human, you need to rest, and if you give without ever giving yourself time to recharge, you won't be able to provide as much as you could otherwise, either now or in the long run..[78]

---

[78] "Dementia, Caregiving, and Controlling Frustration - Family Caregiver Alliance," Family Caregiver Alliance, February 4, 2022, https://www.caregiver.org/resource/dementia-caregiving-and-controlling-frustration/.

Creating a Routine

Routines provide structure, and structure provides expectations that make people feel safe. This feeling of safety is vital for both you and the patient, as dementia changes things quickly and often. The familiarity that comes with a routine brings comfort and calm to a person who is losing their ability to plan, initiate, and complete activities. This also helps them perform activities more easily, giving them a sense of control and continued independence. Also, once a familiar pattern is established, the daily routine is embedded into the long-term memory portion of the brain.

When establishing a routine, start with the basics. When and how does the patient bathe, dress, groom, eat, use the bathroom, and exercise? What are their favorite clothes, foods, and shows? At the point of diagnosis, observe these things so you can help to maintain them. The more you can facilitate activities in line with their pre-dementia life, both hygienic and leisurely, the better.

Gather all the information about their pre-dementia way of life as you can so you can keep things as consistent as possible. It is just as essential to allow the patient to do as much for themselves as they can for as long as they can. Work to maintain routines even as the disease progresses. As they begin to lose abilities, perform tasks together before you take over tasks completely. While doing everything by yourself from the start may be easier, it isn't the best approach for the patient. Small, incremental changes leave fewer surprises, which helps relieve anxiety and minimize undesirable behaviors..[79]

Kendra had the benefit of living only a few minutes from Sheila for years, so she was familiar with Sheila's everyday life. She made a list of all the things she knew about her sister's routine and sat down one day to intentionally take notes on the things she didn't know. She turned this list into a schedule to keep herself on task when overwhelmed and planned to hand it off to Tyler, Meredith, or whoever else would help later on. While doing this provided relief

---

[79] Admin, "The Important of Routine and Familiarity to Persons With Dementia," Alzheimer's Project, June 7, 2020, https://alzheimersproject.org/the-importance-of-routine-and-familiarity-to-persons-with-dementia/.

THE PRACTICAL DEMENTIA CAREGIVER GUIDE

for Kendra, stress could have initially been avoided had she not taken over all the tasks in the beginning out of kindness and selflessness. Doing so caused her to burn out quickly and contributed to Sheila's swift loss of abilities. I'd instructed her to avoid trying to handle all the responsibilities on her own for these reasons. Regardless of how virtuous, or even efficient it feels to absorb all the responsibility, the end result is almost always the same; burnout for the caregiver and perhaps added anxiety for the patient. Everyone benefits from sharing duties from the beginning.

As you create a routine, keep the following in mind:

1. Do the same things at the same time of day in the same order.
2. Include exercise or movement in the routine, like a morning walk.
3. Include mentally therapeutic or engaging activities, like puzzles or music.
4. Keep choices simple. For example, serve the same menu every week, or offer only one or two meal options.
5. Determine what time of day the patient functions best and align the most involved tasks with that time.
6. Keep a calendar and clock visible to the patient so they can keep up with the day and time and know what is coming next.
7. Repetition is good. It helps the patient feel competent.
8. If your loved one needs a caregiver other than you, keep a consistent caregiver rather than rotating caregivers. This helps to build trust and reduce change. It also creates a relationship that makes it easier for caregivers to know if something isn't right with the patient.[80]

---

[80] Esther Heerema Msw, "The Benefits of Routines for People With Dementia," Verywell Health, July 29, 2022, https://www.verywellhealth.com/using-routines-in-dementia-97625.

9. Alert family and friends of visiting time in your routine to keep spontaneity to a minimum..[81]

Please note that as dementia progresses, keeping to an actual time schedule might become more difficult as the person with dementia becomes slower in understanding and staying organized. Meeting a particular time slot with a person in the mid- and later stages of dementia can become challenging for the patient and the caregiver. In these cases, instead of using the exact hours, you can use 'morning time,' 'tea time,' or 'dinner time' to keep the routine schedule.

A Safe Environment

The physical environment of the dementia patient is crucial to their safety and independence. Some modifications may be necessary to help with memory loss, disorientation, coordination, mobility, and security. Only make necessary changes to keep confusion to a minimum. Different considerations are required for indoor environments versus outdoor environments.

The indoor environment should be relaxing and bring happy memories. Lighting is an important factor, so be sure the lighting in the home is sufficient but not too bright, and place nightlights in key places (the bathroom, the hallway, the bedroom) to guide your loved one once it gets dark outside. Consider noise levels (loud noises are annoying to people with dementia), the effects of mirrors, and colors or patterns. Try to eliminate anything the patient may find frightening, like shadows, glare, and reflections.

Floors should be safe, so give attention to slippery floors, loose carpets or rugs, and clutter that could cause the patient to fall. Check the locks, doors, windows, stairs, and balconies for faults that need modification. Make sure the hot water heater is set to a temperature that won't cause burns and that air conditioners and heating are in working order. Consider installing sensor lights or timers if the patient is a night wanderer. Install handrails on both sides of all stairs, and mark glass doors and windows with masking tape. Finally, keep

---

[81] "Daily Care Plan," Alzheimer's Disease and Dementia, n.d., https://www.alz.org/help-support/caregiving/daily-care/daily-care-plan.

the inside of the home at a comfortable temperature, adjust the patient's clothing if the temperature gets too hot or cold, and keep the doors that lead to outside locked at night to keep the patient from leaving the house.

Outdoor areas should also be a safe and relaxing environment where the patient can perform soothing activities. Consider the condition of the garden bed, if there is one, and the possibility of putting water hoses on a timer so your loved one doesn't have to remember to turn them off. If pets are around, ensure they're safe and properly cared for. Fencing should also be safe and locked. However, if there wasn't a fence before, be wary of installing a new one, as it may make the patient feel trapped. Finally, remove obstacles from walking paths, relocate poisonous or spiky plants, and lock up chemicals.

Next, let's consider specific areas of the home for safety.

Kitchens

Safety is essential here, as it's easy to get cut or burned in a kitchen. Adhere to the general rule of allowing the patient to stay as independent as possible for as long as possible while also trying to keep things familiar. If you need to replace an appliance, try to keep it as close to the original as possible. Consider appliances with safety features, like automatic off switches and the placement of cords away from water or heating sources. Label cabinets so the patient can find things easily and leave the most commonly used items out for easy access. Reduce the temperature of the water heater at the source. Depending on the state of the patient, you may need to remove or lock up sharp knives, toxic products, and medicines.

Living rooms

Make sure the walkways are safe and consider rearranging furniture if necessary. Provide a sturdy, comfortable chair for the patient to get in and out of easily and consider waterproofing it in case your loved one deals with incontinence. Remove unstable furniture like rocking chairs or items with wheels, cover sharp edges, and remove loose floor coverings or rugs. If there are pieces that are easy to trip over, like low coffee tables, remove those, too.

Be mindful of sharp or breakable objects but leave safe ornaments that bring back happy memories.

Bedrooms

It should be easy for the patient to get in and out of bed, so consider the bed's height and firmness. Soft night lights can help the patient find the bathroom. Make sure the flooring is safe by removing loose carpets and rugs.

Bathrooms

Set up the bathroom so the patient can be as independent as possible while respecting their privacy as much as possible. Consider labeling the toilet and doors, installing grab rails and rubber mats in the shower, and locking away potentially dangerous items like razors, hair dryers, and cleaning products. You might need to remove locks so the patient doesn't lock themselves in. Finally, find a way to make the temperature in the bathroom comfortable, if possible, like providing a fan or space heater.

Laundry rooms

Keep the laundry room as simple and clutter-free as possible. If the patient can no longer use this area safely, lock up poisonous products, store the iron, and turn off the washer and dryer at the wall.

As dementia progresses, memories will fade, including memories of how to get around the home. Pay attention to what the patient forgets so you know what memory aids to use. For example, if they forget daily tasks, write them on a whiteboard in a central location. If they forget their keys, hang them on a hook near the door. You can also consider technological supportive aids such as phone reminders, alarms, and audio messages. These support aids can be as sophisticated as a GPS system that helps locate a person if they get lost.[82]

---

[82] Healthdirect Australia, "Creating a Calming, Helpful Home for People With Dementia," Healthdirect, n.d., https://www.healthdirect.gov.au/creating-a-calming-home-for-people-with-dementia.

Take Action

The keys to creating a safe environment are prevention, simplification, and patience while balancing safety and independence. Consider all the changes taking place in the life of your loved one and make the appropriate accommodations. Use this checklist from alzheimer.ca to help note what changes to make in the home.[83]:

HOME SAFETY CHECKLIST	Yes	No
Do I need to store the rugs and secure the carpet to prevent falls?		
Are the stairways safe for the person I am caring for?		
Is the person with dementia able to use the electrical appliances in the kitchen and bathroom safely?		
Should the water heater temperature be lowered?		
Are there any medications, cleaning substances, or gardening chemicals that should be locked away?		
Do I need to be there when the person with dementia has a cigarette, or should I hide the lighter and matches?		
Should I lock some of the doors, or should I change the location of the locks?		
Should I consider installing safety equipment in the bathroom (e.g., grab bars, an elevated toilet seat, and a non-slip mat)?		
Does the lighting sufficiently eliminate shadows that may cause confusion?		
Are there items that confuse the person with Dementia (e.g., pictures, mirrors)?		

---

[83] "Making Your Environment Safe," Alzheimer Society of Canada, n.d., https://alzheimer.ca/en/help-support/im-caring-person-living-dementia/ensuring-safety-security/making-your-environment-safe.

Preparation is key. Take the time to prepare the patient's living space to give them the safest, most comfortable environment possible. It's just as important to do the mental work to prepare yourself for the frustrating times ahead. Since the changes in the patient's memory and functional ability are usually gradual, their needs and environmental adjustments should change gradually, as well. Preparing for these adjustments today can help to alleviate some of the stress to come.

Take a few minutes to fill out the **Home Safety Checklist** so you'll know which projects to tend to for your loved one's safety. Additionally, choose an activity, like journaling or meditation, to do each day for 10 minutes to strengthen your mental fortitude. Doing so will take you far in your communication and interactions from here on out.

In the coming chapter we'll explore tactics that will help you communicate with your loved one from the early stages of their diagnosis all the way to the late stages of dementia.

CHAPTER 6

Exploring Ways to Communicate

It didn't take long for Sheila's health to begin to deteriorate. She still knew who Kendra was, and although she had become comfortable with Tyler when he visited, she couldn't remember his name. Before long, she was forgetting more and more, like when to change clothes or which medication to take. However, what Kendra found most challenging was how difficult it was becoming to communicate with Sheila.

Communication Challenges

Communication is key in any relationship. This is especially the case when it comes to caring for someone with dementia. Good communication will be a lifesaver for you as the caregiver, and it will help the patient maintain a sense of self, relationships, and quality of life. While it's true that conversations will become more difficult as the disease progresses, effective communication is still possible.

From the early stages to the late stages, dementia will progressively make speaking more difficult, causing frustration for everyone involved. The patient may increasingly have trouble finding the right words to express themselves, their speech may become repetitive, or they may say one thing when they mean something else. These changes can trigger negative emotions in your loved one, making their behavior a challenge. Importantly, language difficulties are unpredictable. They can change from day to day or even depending on the time of day. Language can become more of a barrier if the patient is tired, in pain, not feeling well, or in uncomfortable surroundings. The type of dementia the patient has can also be a factor. For example, Frontotemporal Dementia often brings on language challenges earlier than other types of dementia. Changes you might see, other than the patient's loss of ability to find the words they're looking for, can be their using related words (saying "comb" instead of "brush"), substituting words ("the thing we ride in" instead of "car"), using words that have no meaning, using a mishmash of words, or returning to the language the patient learned first if they speak more than one language. Additionally, vision or hearing problems can compound communicative difficulties.

As the patient loses their ability to communicate, they also lose the ability to make caregivers aware of their needs. There is a feeling of entrapment that comes with wanting to share information but being unable to. This loss of the capability to say how they feel and what they want can lead to depression, which expedites complications of dementia. Someone who was previously a lively communicator may feel as though they've lost themselves to the disease. And it can be unnerving or even embarrassing for the caregiver when they can't understand what the patient is trying to convey, or conversely, when what they are trying to convey isn't heard or understood.

The frustration that accompanies the inability to communicate can irritate the patient and trigger inappropriate behavior. In addition to frustration, they might long for the social stimulation they enjoyed before. At this point, isolation and loneliness become major issues. Therefore, it is essential for loved ones to go the extra mile to maintain meaningful connections.

Since dementia impacts how people think, it can also affect their ability to follow a conversation. Patients may need help focusing on a conversation or understanding what others have said. They may think more slowly or struggle to organize words into an appropriate reply. You may also notice them moving readily from topic to topic. Finally, changes in communication can result in inappropriate comments, repetitive questions, or believing things that aren't true..[84]

Communication issues can also be a side effect of medication. Note that if there's a sudden change in your loved one's behavior over just a matter of hours, delirium might be the cause. Delirium is the rapid onset of confusion and altered consciousness, often accompanied by hallucinations and agitation, that can result from various medical, surgical, or psychiatric conditions such as infection, heart or lung issues, medication side effects, etc. It is considered a medical emergency that requires immediate attention.

Practically Speaking; Communication Strategies

When Kendra considered placing Sheila in a long-term care facility, we discussed all the benefits and challenges of the decision. If Kendra were to move in with Sheila, Sheila would feel safer and more secure in the familiarity of her own home. Staying in her own home would ensure familiar surroundings whenever she started wandering, and Kendra could quickly get to her sister to help in an environment she knew well. But Kendra was exhausted, and Sheila's medical needs were beginning to feel like more than she was qualified to handle on her own. On the other hand, if Sheila were to go into a care facility, she would have the around-the-clock medical care that she needed, and her environment might even be more secure, reducing Sheila's ability to wander off the premises and go missing. However, this would mean a higher travel burden for Kendra since the closest long-term care facility was an hour away. It would mean fewer opportunities for the sisters to engage in daily activities together and connect in the way they'd been connecting since receiving the diagnosis.

Kendra feared that if the staff at the facility didn't follow the routine she'd work to establish, couldn't play word games with Sheila, or didn't tend to her with the same care, Sheila's health would deteriorate. She would feel more

---

[84] "Dementia and Language," Alzheimer's Society, n.d., https://www.alzheimers.org.uk/about-dementia/symptoms-and-diagnosis/symptoms/dementia-and-language#content-start.

isolated, less stimulated, less connected to Kendra, and more agitated, which would cause more frustration for everyone.

I shared a technological development with Kendra that has made connection from afar a little easier: the telepresence robot. This robot allows family members or friends to see the person with dementia through a mobile two-way screen. In the absence of physical presence, the robot provides a way for the patient and their loved ones to see each other in real-time without the need for anyone to manage the robot, as it is freestanding and wheel based. It has self-driving sensors and microphones, enabling verbal communication. Since it's mobile, it can move throughout the facility, which means the family can communicate with the patient about whatever is happening around them. Additionally, this robot can be used without the help of a worker from the care facility. It can provide a sense of presence for both the patient and the caregiver.[85] While nothing tops the physical presence of a loved one, technological options are making things easier. Kendra kept this information in her memory bank in case she might need it later.

Kendra wasn't ready to put Sheila in a long-term care facility, so she became extra vigilant in her efforts to continue to care for her at home. She noticed that Sheila's language and behavior were much better first thing in the morning rather than in the afternoon, so they switched their standing weekly lunch date to a breakfast outing instead. When Sheila was tired, sad, or in pain, it became harder for her to talk. She couldn't easily let Kendra know what was going on when talking was difficult, which would make Sheila angry. When she became angry, she was mean to Kendra. Kendra would become cold and bite her tongue in an effort to not offend, but the look on her face made it clear to Sheila that Kendra was unhappy. Sheila would try to take medicine on her own whenever she was in pain without considering the appropriate time between doses or how the drug might interact with her other prescriptions. Kendra once caught Sheila trying to take medicine she didn't need. When Kendra took it away, Sheila yelled and threw things at her, accusing Kendra of treating her

---

[85] Wendy Moyle, "Grand Challenge of Maintaining Meaningful Communication in Dementia Care," *Frontiers in Dementia* 2 (March 3, 2023), https://doi.org/10.3389/frdem.2023.1137897.

like a child. Kendra didn't yell back, but she squinted her eyes and burst into tears, which made Sheila even more upset.

As Kendra tried to manage Sheila's pain and emotions, her own mental health took a hit. They didn't have much family around, and the family they did have were busy with their own lives and couldn't commit to the kind of assistance Kendra desperately needed. Ultimately, Kendra wasn't sure how much more she could take. When she came to me about this, we sat down and reviewed her patterns when communicating with her sister. We saw several changes Kendra could implement that turned out to be helpful.

As dementia gets worse, the patient will notice that they can't communicate like they did before.[86] This can cause stress for them and their caregivers, and it means having to communicate more using body language, physical contact, facial expressions, drawing, singing, or technology.[87] If you're away from your loved one, face-to-face communication through video calls can help ease these difficulties.[88]

When making adjustments to your own modes of communication, keep the following tips in mind:

- Try to avoid negative body language, like sighs or furrowed eyebrows.

- Mindfulness of tone and voice pitch are also important coping strategies for the caregiver. A calm tone of voice, focused sentences, adequate response time to questions or comments, and orienting labels that connect names to relationships (*"Your friend, Mindy, came over today,"* or *"Your dog, Rex, is ready for a walk."*) are essential.

- Avoid competing with other noise, like the television or radio.

---

[86] "Dementia and Language."
[87] "Non-verbal Communication and Dementia," Alzheimer's Society, January 19, 2022, https://www.alzheimers.org.uk/about-dementia/symptoms-and-diagnosis/symptoms/non-verbal-communication-and-dementia.
[88] "Communicating and Dementia," Alzheimer's Society, n.d., https://www.alzheimers.org.uk/about-dementia/symptoms-and-diagnosis/symptoms/communicating-and-dementia.

- Stand still while talking to give the patient an opportunity to focus on what you're saying instead of competing with your movements.

- Do not argue with them, order them around, tell them what they can't or shouldn't do, speak to them in a condescending manner, ask a barrage of questions, or speak about them like they don't exist.

The Alzheimer's Association recommends caretakers always approach the patient from the front, look at them when speaking, and use the same physical touch or call their name before talking to them. Do not try to guess what they want to say when they attempt to speak, and if possible, encourage them to write down what they're trying to tell you if they struggle to find the words. Pictures of items they use often can also be helpful, as they can point to the image instead of dealing with the frustration of trying to figure out what to say. There is no need to correct the patient if they are wrong. Remember, a calm, low-anxiety environment is the goal..[89]

Other strategies include validation therapy, which acknowledges the feelings behind the patient's words and behavior, even if the information is wrong. Sheila had begun retelling the same stories, and each time she told a story, a detail would change. At first, Kendra would try to correct her (*"No, Sheila. You took a picture with the senator of Vermont on vacation at the Grand Canyon, not at Mount Rushmore"*). After a while, Kendra realized being right made no difference, and pushing her sister on the details only caused friction. Another strategy is music therapy, which involves playing songs the patient enjoys to unlock positive memories. Sheila's favorite musician was the cellist Yo-Yo Ma, so Kendra played his music every day during their morning routine.

Reminiscing is another way of bringing memories to mind, and it's useful even if the patient can no longer communicate. This strategy is most effective when the memories are positive, so be sensitive to the patient's reactions to what you say. Finally, a legacy project, like a chronological, visual diary of the patient's

---

[89] Silva Banovic, Lejla Junuzovic Zunic, and Osman Sinanovic, "Communication Difficulties as a Result of Dementia," Materia socio-medica, October 2018, https://www.ncbi.nlm.nih.gov/pmc/articles/PMC6195406/.

THE PRACTICAL DEMENTIA CAREGIVER GUIDE

life, can be an informative way to help everyone caring for the patient learn more about their life and to spark positive memories for the patient.[90] With this in mind, Kendra gathered photos from her home and Sheila's, bought a large scrapbook, and organized the images in the book from oldest to most recent. She labeled each section by year and added short notes to the pictures as she recalled the details. When Sheila was feeling good, Kendra would sit next to her with the scrapbook and flip through at Sheila's pace while they relived the memories on the pages.

As with all other aspects of your loved one's care, communication should be executed with a tailored approach according to what works best for the patient. Here are a few more valuable tips to remember:

- Pay attention to the best time of day for the patient to communicate and try to ask important questions only then.

- Before trying to talk, make sure all their needs are met. For example, ensure they're not hungry, thirsty, or in pain.

- If the roles were reversed, how would you want others to approach you? Keep this in mind when communicating with your loved one.

- Avoid communication if you are in a rush. If you don't have the time to allow your loved one all the time they need to express their thoughts and understand your responses, save the conversation for later.

- Take notes on which tactics previously helped facilitate good communication so you can rely on those later.

- Allow the patient to express their feelings if they're upset. Don't be dismissive or try to find the right thing to say. Being there and showing you care by listening is enough.

---

[90] Department of Health & Human Services, "Dementia - Communication," Better Health Channel, n.d., https://www.betterhealth.vic.gov.au/health/conditionsandtreatments/dementia-communication.

- Speak clearly and succinctly but avoid talking to the patient like they're a child.

- Speak conversationally instead of formally, and don't be afraid to include the patient in conversations with others.

- If they don't understand what you're saying, express yourself in a different way. Change your wording, shorten your sentences, use pictures, or utilize more body language and gestures.

- Keep it light. If they or you make a mistake in the process of navigating this new communication, there's no harm in that. Laughter is still a powerful medicine.[91]

If verbal communication is no longer an option, non-verbal communication, which is any communication without words, is an effective alternative. Gestures, facial expressions, and body language may become the main ways you communicate with your loved one as their dementia progresses. This may be especially necessary if the patient has reverted to a native language that you don't speak or understand. Art therapy, music, poetry, and drama can be effective modes of communication. During the later stages of the disease, if the patient cannot speak, caretakers can still talk to them and communicate with gentle touch like handholding. If you rely on non-verbal communication, remember:

- Physical contact can be comforting, like an arm around the shoulder or hand holding.

- Sitting too closely or standing over the patient can feel intimidating, so try to give appropriate space and sit at eye level.

- Avoid sudden movements, harsh facial expressions, or a rough tone of voice, all of which can be upsetting to the patient.

---

[91] "How to Communicate With a Person With Dementia," Alzheimer's Society, December 20, 2021, https://www.alzheimers.org.uk/about-dementia/symptoms-and-diagnosis/symptoms/how-to-communicate-dementia#content-start.

- Make sure your words and body language match. If you're speaking of positive memories, smiling helps to reinforce what you're saying.

- Try to understand what the patient is saying with their own body language.

- Use visual prompts, like pictures or cue cards, to communicate objects or ideas the patient may no longer be able to name.[92]

Non-verbal communication is powerful for several reasons. Firstly, it encourages self-expression and fosters a sense of trust. Also, eye contact and touch help form bonds and boost confidence. Secondly, it prevents confusion and agitation by giving the patient a firmer grasp of your words. Thirdly, it helps convey emotions so the patient can accurately place your intent, avoiding unnecessary confusion and arguments. Finally, it soothes ailments. Physical touch stimulates oxytocin, which lowers stress, reduces pain, and increases blood flow.[93]

Once Kendra understood how powerful touch could be in her sister's care plan, she became intentional about touching Sheila during their time together. She would take a deep breath and put her arm around her sister's shoulder when she sensed Sheila's frustration. She would place her hand on Sheila's arm when she grew tired and give her hand massages in the evenings before bed.

Oxytocin, the "care and connection" hormone, can play a significant role in improving the mental health of dementia patients. In fact, research has found that five minutes of hand massage can decrease stress hormones and anxiety. One study of 68 nursing home residents found that patients who received 10 minutes of massage displayed significantly reduced anxiety than those who didn't. Physical touch can also be implemented through hair combing or

---

[92] "Non-Verbal Communication and Dementia."
[93] "Why Nonverbal Communication Is Vital When Caring for Seniors With Dementia," Home Care Assistance Winnipeg, January 21, 2022, https://www.homecareassistancewinnipeg.ca/importance-of-non-verbal-communication-in-dementia-care/.

brushing, manicures, hugs, high-fives, massage therapy, handshakes, or gentle pats on the arm..[94]

Interestingly, physical touch can pull out positive memories, and improving the mood reduces agitation and unease for up to an hour. Dementia patients, especially those in care facilities, can often feel disconnected from their surroundings. Physical touch helps to ground them. Additionally, seniors with memory loss conditions often suffer from touch deprivation, which increases feelings of depression, anxiety, insecurity, isolation, and decreased sensory awareness. Touch gives physical and emotional connection, directly affecting mental health and general well-being. Even after memories fade, patients can still recognize gentle touch, which boosts positive emotions.

Since touch therapy reduces agitation, dissociation, and restlessness, it can also decrease the behaviors that stem from these feelings, such as wandering, combativeness, resistance to help, and verbal outbursts. Adding touch to the patient's daily routine can foster a sense of safety and pleasantness, allowing your loved one to feel secure and helping you feel more in control of a volatile situation..[95]

To recap, here are a few ways to effectively use non-verbal communication with a dementia patient:

- Look them in the eyes when speaking to them.
- Use gentle touch as a means of connection and to evoke feelings of safety.
- Use pictures and photos of objects they can point to when they can't find the words to use in everyday conversation.

---

[94] Why touch is important in alzheimer's care | blog | right at ..., accessed March 13, 2024, https://www.rightathome.net/boston-north/blog/touch-important-in-alzheimers-care.
[95] Carly Dodd Pacifica Senior Living, "Touch & Memory Care: The Power Of Touch Therapy for Dementia Residents," *Pacifica Senior Living* (blog), November 2, 2023,
https://blog.pacificaseniorliving.com/blog/touch-memory-care-the-power-of-touch-therapy-for-dementia-residents.

- Give them hand massages to convey connectedness and reduce anxiety.

- Use body language to reinforce the message you're trying to get across.

- Use pleasant facial expressions to help them understand your tone.

- Don't sit or stand too closely to the patient, as this may feel intimidating.

- Use music therapy to elicit positive memories.

Take Action

The communication barrier caused by dementia can be disheartening, but it is a very real indicator of the seriousness of this disease. Take a few moments to note how you've seen your loved one's communication abilities diminish. After that, write down any questions you have for your doctor concerning your loved one's symptoms or how you can best implement the solutions you've seen in this chapter. When other caregivers come into the picture, it's important to be able to provide them with as much information about the patient as possible. Alzheimer's Society has a simple "This is me" form that serves as a record of personal information. It includes how the patient communicates, the difficulties they commonly run into, and ways support staff can best serve them.

Scan the QR code below to download the form.

https://www.alzheimers.org.uk/sites/default/files/2020-03/this_is_me_1553.pdf

Keep in mind that several different factors can influence the patient's ability to communicate, including the stage of dementia, the time of day, medication, or even how the patient is feeling at the time. Your ability to notice what triggers these changes will significantly help determine how to deal with them. The strategies in this chapter are proven to help make these challenges more manageable. As you work to implement these strategies, be sure to share this information with everyone involved in your loved one's care so they can do the same.

As you're likely already aware, communication is not the only challenge that comes with dementia. Changes in behavior can be incredibly taxing on the caregiver. Fortunately, tactics are available to help deal with this, too. The next chapter will walk you through what these behaviors might entail, give tips to deal with a variety of complex behaviors, and show the best ways to get through challenging days.

CHAPTER 7

Dealing With Challenging Days

Whenever Kendra thought she was catching her breath, something new would take it away again.

Sheila's angry outbursts had become commonplace, and Kendra was coping, but then came the paranoia, refusal to eat, shadowing, and—scariest of all—the wandering. At Sheila's appointments, Kendra would cry in frustration as she explained the challenges that were coming in waves. Sheila would begin to cry when she saw Kendra crying. I empathized with their feelings, as this was a scene I'd witnessed countless times over the years.

Your loved one is going to change. Their personality and behaviors will shift, and it will be in your best interest to meet these challenges with patience, compassion, flexibility, and creativity. Remember, these changes are due to fundamental alterations in their brain, so it's best not to take personally what they say and do. Follow these guidelines to help navigate these transitions.

1. **Know that you cannot change the person.** There's nothing you can do about the effects dementia is having on the patient's brain. The disorder is shaping their new self; it's not by choice. You'll likely be met with resistance if you try to change behaviors. Things will be easier for everyone if you try accommodating the behavior instead of

controlling it. For example, if the patient insists on sleeping on the couch rather than in the bed like they have done all their life, provide them with a pillow and a blanket to help them get comfortable on the couch, instead of forcing them into the bed. You'll be much more successful when you focus on your own responses and the physical environment instead of the patient's behavior.

2. **Check with the doctor early.** Where there is a behavioral problem, there might be an underlying medical cause, like severe pain, a urinary tract infection, or medication side effects. In some cases, like incontinence or hallucinations, medications might help.

3. **Behavior has a purpose.** Dementia patients often cannot verbally express their needs, so they may do things we cannot understand. For example, if they start to take all the dishes out of the cabinets each day, they may be trying to fulfill a need to be productive. When you notice strange behaviors, think a step past the behavior, consider what they may be really trying to accomplish, and try to accommodate that need.

4. **Behavior has triggers.** There is a reason behind all behaviors. It could be a word, an action, or even a change of environment. Notice these triggers so you can take different approaches or implement different consequences for problem behaviors.

5. **What works today may not work tomorrow.** Dementia is progressive, which means the disease is constantly changing. Since it's ever-changing, so are its accompanying behaviors. What worked yesterday might not work today. You'll have to tap into your creativity and flexibility to keep up with strategies that help curb problematic actions.

6. **Get support from others.** Always remember that you are not alone. There are millions of people dealing with dementia each day. It's so pervasive that support groups and online communities have been established so you don't have to do it alone. Find a group,

organizations, services, or individuals that can offer advice. A great resource is the **Family Care Navigator**, a tool that helps family caregivers locate public, private, and non-profit programs and services near their loved ones.

Scan the QR code below to access the Family Care Navigator.

https://www.caregiver.org/family-care-navigator

Now, let's examine behaviors you might encounter and ways to help deal with them.

New Behaviors to Deal With

Wandering

It's common for dementia patients to walk around aimlessly. They may no longer recognize familiar places or are becoming confused about their location. Wandering can happen at any stage of the disease. Six in ten people will wander at least once, and many patients will develop it as a habit.[96] It must be taken seriously, as the patient can easily end up in a dangerous position. If a patient begins to exhibit the following behaviors, they may be at risk for wandering:

- Returning from a regular activity later than usual
- Forgetting directions to familiar places

---

[96] "Wandering," Alzheimer's Disease and Dementia, accessed March 13, 2024, https://www.alz.org/help-support/caregiving/stages-behaviors/wandering.

- Talking about doing things they no longer do, like going to work
- Trying to go home even if they're already at home
- Pacing, repetitive movements, or other restless behaviors
- Having trouble locating familiar places, like the bathroom
- Asking about the whereabouts of people who are no longer around
- Becoming nervous in crowded areas.[97]

Dementia patients wander for different reasons. They might be trying to fill a physical need, like hunger or exercise. They might be bored or looking for something or someone. Here's how you can help:

- Make time for regular exercise to minimize restlessness in the patient.
- Assess the locks in the home and replace them if necessary. Install locks that require a key and consider placing the locks above or below eye level, as many patients won't think to look beyond eye level.
- Place child-safe plastic covers on doorknobs to prevent them from easily leaving.
- Consider installing a home security system or giving the patient a watch or other device with a GPS tracking system.
- Have them wear an ID bracelet and sew ID labels into their clothes to be easily identifiable in case they go missing.
- Let neighbors know about your loved one's wandering behaviors so they can be on the lookout.[98]

---

[97] "Wandering."
[98] "Caregiver's Guide to Understanding Dementia Behaviors - Family Caregiver Alliance," Family Caregiver Alliance, March 9, 2024, https://www.caregiver.org/resource/caregivers-guide-understanding-dementia-behaviors/.

It's important to be proactive when this behavior appears. Make a list of places the patient may wander off to, keep a recent photo available to show to first responders, and enroll your loved one in the Alzheimer's Association's **wandering response service**, a nationwide service that helps facilitate the safe return of those living with dementia or suffering from a medical emergency. If your loved one disappears, start searching for them immediately. Be aware that many wandering people are found within 1.5 miles of where they disappeared. Search where they've wandered in the past; check landscapes, as many are found in the brush; and if you haven't found them in 15 minutes, alert the authorities.[99]

Scan the QR code below to access the below Alzheimer's Association's wandering response service.

https://www.alz.org/help-support/caregiving/safety/medicalert-with-24-7-wandering-support

Kendra didn't know that when Sheila started talking about what she'd done at work one day or asked about their great-grandmother, she was at risk of wandering. One morning, Kendra woke up and went to check on Sheila, but Sheila wasn't there. Fortunately, she had gotten in the habit of taking pictures of Sheila on her good days, so when she called the police after realizing Sheila wasn't on the premises, she had a photo from the day before to show them. After the incident, Kendra purchased a watch with a GPS tracker for Sheila. She bought herself a matching watch so Sheila wouldn't protest. She attached a small alarm to each door so she could hear her sister come and go, and she let the neighbors know that this behavior had begun. Those measures were of

---

[99] "Wandering."

tremendous help, as that was the last time Sheila was able to wander off, but it wasn't the last time she tried.

Incontinence

Incontinence is the loss of bladder or bowel control, and it often occurs as dementia progresses. This might happen because the patient has forgotten where the bathroom is, or they can't get to it in time.[100] The patient may have trouble communicating, making them unable to tell someone they need to go. They may not be able to react to the sensation of needing to use the bathroom. They may refuse the help they need to use the bathroom. And if they have an accident, they may try to hide their soiled clothes.[101] Either way, incontinence is embarrassing, so it's important for the caregiver to display a sense of understanding to help the patient maintain their dignity.

Some helpful tactics to deal with incontinence are as follows:

- Establish a routine for using the bathroom and keep the schedule.
- Schedule fluid intake to balance hydration and toilet time. Limit fluids before bedtime.
- Use signs to point the patient in the direction of the bathroom.
- Leave a portable commode next to the bed.
- Utilize incontinence pads if necessary.
- Make sure the patient wears clothes that are easy to remove, like those with elastic waistbands instead of buttons and zippers.[102]

Agitation

Your loved one may appear irritable, sleepless, or verbally and/or physically aggressive. All of these behaviors fall under the umbrella of agitation, and they

---

[100] "Caregiver's Guide to Understanding Dementia Behaviors - Family Caregiver Alliance."
[101] https://www.alzheimers.org.uk/get-support/daily-living/toilet-problems-continence
[102] "Caregiver's Guide to Understanding Dementia Behaviors - Family Caregiver Alliance."

progress as dementia does. Agitation can be triggered by the environment, changes in routine, fear, or fatigue, but most often, it happens when the patient feels like they lack control.[103] When your loved one becomes agitated:

- Ask for their permission before you do anything else.
- Listen to their frustration so you can understand their triggers.
- Provide reassurance with phrases like, "You're safe here."
- Do something with them that will reduce their anxiety, like playing a game or taking a walk.
- Keep your composure.[104]
- Reduce noise, clutter, or people in the room.
- Reduce foods or drinks that cause a spike in energy, like caffeine.
- Try gentle touch, music, or a walk.[105]

Repetitive Speech or Actions (Perseveration)

Perseveration is the act of repeating a word, statement, question, or activity over and over. While it's harmless for the patient, it can be a source of frustration for the caregiver. This behavior is triggered by anxiety, boredom, fear, or environmental factors. Here are a few things you can do in response when the patient perseverates:

- Provide comforting words and touch.
- Offer a distraction, like a snack.
- Redirect their attention towards another activity.

---

[103] "Caregiver's Guide to Understanding Dementia Behaviors - Family Caregiver Alliance."
[104] "How to Help When Dementia Leads to Agitation," n.d., https://www.psychiatry.org/news-room/apa-blogs/how-to-help-when-dementia-leads-to-agitation.
[105] "Caregiver's Guide to Understanding Dementia Behaviors - Family Caregiver Alliance."

- Don't start a conversation that will confuse them even more.

- Pay attention to behaviors that accompany repetition, such as pulling at clothing that may indicate another need like urination or defecation.[106]

Paranoia

Your loved one can start to experience delusions. They can be convinced that someone is trying to hurt them or take something from them. These feelings of being threatened can come from nowhere and make the patient suspicious of everyone around them. The patient may feel like they're being watched or that someone is out to get them, and they may jump to conclusions with nothing to back up their feelings. This is one of the more challenging behaviors for caregivers, as the patient may treat you like an enemy when you've done nothing to harm them. Sadly, you may not be able to convince them otherwise. Common delusions include theft (losing something and thinking someone stole it), the belief that someone close to them is trying to hurt them (thinking someone bringing them food is trying to poison them), or not believing their home is their home. When you notice these behaviors:

- Acknowledge their distress and listen to them. Encourage them to talk through what they're feeling.

- Try to gently offer an explanation different from what they think is true but reassure them that their thoughts are being taken seriously.

- Control the environment. If they think someone's trying to poison them, get their food from somewhere or someone else.

- Try not to take their accusations personally.

---

[106] "Caregiver's Guide to Understanding Dementia Behaviors - Family Caregiver Alliance."

- Don't validate their delusions, but don't try to correct or argue with them either. Find or make up a harmless explanation that would be believable to the patient and calm them down.

- Seek out the reason for the accusation. If they're accusing someone of theft, try to find the missing item and create a consistent place for it.

- Don't always assume the patient's accusations are untrue..[107]

On one occasion, Tyler popped up during a three-day weekend to visit with Sheila and Kendra. He brought food and offered some to Sheila, but she refused to eat it and accused Tyler of trying to poison her. Not knowing what else to do, Kendra ate some of the food in front of Sheila to prove it wasn't poisonous. She later pulled Tyler aside to explain all the new things Sheila had started doing since he'd last visited. Tyler then decided not to bring anything he would directly present to his aunt. Instead, he would give any treats to Kendra and let her be the one to give them to Sheila.

Sleeplessness/Sundowning

Sundowning refers to increased restlessness, agitation, or confusion that worsens in dementia patients as daylight fades. It can continue into the night, making it harder for them to sleep or stay in bed. It can be caused by exhaustion from the day and changes in the patient's biological clock that confuse day and night. Other causes may include unmet needs like hunger or thirst, depression, medical illness, change of environment, pain, or boredom. It also commonly happens when patient is admitted to the hospital. As with all behaviors, try to find the root cause and listen to the patient's frustrations. Be a source of reassurance for them that everything will be okay. The same tactics that work for other behaviors also work here, so reduce noise and clutter in their environment and distract them with an activity or snack. Additionally, you can:

---

[107] "Delusions, Paranoia and Dementia," Alzheimer's Society, February 26, 2021, https://www.alzheimers.org.uk/about-dementia/symptoms-and-diagnosis/delusions.

- Make the early evening a quiet time for them.

- Adjust lighting in their home by letting in natural light during the day and using softer light in the evening. It's important to constantly let them know the time of the day.

- If they are temporarily in an unfamiliar environment (like a hospital) or have just relocated, keep reminding them the date, time, and place.

- Avoid alcohol or caffeine, which may add to confusion or cause a surge of energy.

- Avoid overloading their schedule.

To prevent sundowning:

- Have your loved one go outside or sit by a window during the day. This can help adjust their body's clock.

- Make sure the patient exercises each day.

- If they take naps, ensure they're not too long or too late.

- Aim for you and your loved one to get enough sleep at night.[108]

Eating/Nutrition

Dementia patients may find eating difficult due to loss of appetite or memory. They might forget how to chew and swallow, or their environment might become a distraction to the task of eating. Pain and discomfort, insufficient physical activity, and embarrassment due to the newfound struggles might also contribute to their refusal to eat. Dry mouth, gum disease, or ill-fitting dentures may be a culprit. Furthermore, the patient might mix up the functions of the tools at the table. For example, they may pour juice into a bowl or try to eat

---

[108] "Tips for Coping With Sundowning," National Institute on Aging, n.d., https://www.nia.nih.gov/health/alzheimers-changes-behavior-and-communication/tips-coping-sundowning#:~:text=Late%20afternoon%20and%20early%20evening,tired%20caregivers%20need%20a%20break.

THE PRACTICAL DEMENTIA CAREGIVER GUIDE

hot cereal with a knife. The opposite may also be true; dementia may cause an increase in appetite or a craving for sweet foods. Also, be wary about swallowing dysfunction, a common condition that can appear with aging, dementia, or other medical diseases. If your loved one coughs or chokes often while eating or drinking, have them checked by a speech and swallow specialist. Swallowing dysfunction can lead to food going into the airways, which can cause a lung infection and dangerously low oxygen levels.

Scheduling and proactivity will make mealtime less of a struggle for the patient and caregiver. Some helpful tips include:

- Checking with the doctor to ensure their loss of or increase in appetite isn't due to a treatable cause, like depression

- Offering meals at regular times each day and making sure the meals are balanced

- Making mealtime calm and relaxing and preparing foods that are familiar and enjoyable to the patient

- Offering the patient five to six small meals each day, including healthy snacks

- Staying up to date on dental appointments to make sure no problems are contributing to mouth pain

- Serving one course at a time and removing anything distracting from the table, like decorations or extra utensils

- Offering finger foods and fluids to make the process of eating easier.[109]

Most proactivity takes practical thinking. When Sheila began struggling to feed herself, Kendra was distraught. She didn't think she could continue to care for her sister if she was unable to eat. I told her that before we did anything else, she should make an appointment to see a dentist. They saw the doctor the next

---

[109] Department of Health & Human Services, "Dementia - Eating," Better Health Channel, n.d., https://www.betterhealth.vic.gov.au/health/conditionsandtreatments/dementia-eating.

day and found that Sheila was refusing to eat because she had chipped a tooth, which made eating painful. Kendra sighed in relief. Although handling a chipped tooth came with its own challenges, it was an easy enough problem to fix quickly.

For further information, scan the QR code below to download a free copy of my book **Nourishing the Mind: A Caregiver's Guide to Diet and Nutrition for Dementia.**

https://savvyscrolls.net/dementia

Bathing

Because of the patient's declining abilities, bathing can be physically challenging. Because bathing is a vulnerable act, it can be emotionally challenging. Additionally, visual deficits and depth perception problems can make bathing dangerous and uncomfortable. The patient may not want assistance with such a private activity. They may express this verbally or through resisting, making the process difficult for them and the caregiver. Figuring out what works for a successful bath time is a process of trial and error. Here are some helpful tips:

- Prepare the bathroom in advance by gathering the necessary supplies, providing a comfortable environment with padding or towels on cold surfaces, monitoring the water temperature for safety and comfort, and putting objects like towels and soap within reach of the patient.

- Help the patient feel like they're in control by giving them choices about bath time, having them play a role in the process (they can hold the washcloth or shampoo), not forcing a bath if they resist, allowing them to get in a shallow tub of water before filling it all the way up, or letting them enter the tub or shower wearing a towel to reduce embarrassment. Always keep their dignity top of mind.

- Adapt the bathing process by keeping bath time at the same time each day, using simple phrases to coach them through the process ("*Sit here. Wash your neck. Here's the soap.*") and demonstrating the action for the patient so they don't get confused. Use specialized products, like towels with pockets for the soap, if possible.

- Consider alternatives to bathing, like washing one body part each day, washing the hair at a different time from bath time, giving sponge baths between full bath days, or using wet wipes. You may have to change your standards from what you're used to, but the most important thing is ensuring the patient is clean while keeping friction to a minimum.

- Keep after-bath care in mind. Check for rashes and sores, make sure the patient is seated when drying and dressing them, thoroughly pat them dry instead of rubbing them dry, apply lotion to keep the skin soft, and use cornstarch or powder under the breasts and in skin folds.[110]

Dressing

To a healthy person, getting dressed is a task that can usually be performed on autopilot. But to the dementia patient the struggle with balance, coordination, recognition of the steps in the process, vision changes, medicinal side effects, or depression can make getting dressed a complicated and frustrating task. To help the patient:

- Use gestures and speak slowly to assist them in dressing independently.

---

[110] "Bathing," Alzheimer's Disease and Dementia, n.d., https://www.alz.org/help-support/caregiving/daily-care/bathing.

- Set out their clothes in the order they need to put them on.
- Reduce distractions in the room and keep the room quiet and pleasant.
- Discuss their comfort level regarding privacy to best gauge how to help.
- Label clothing drawers for accessible location of items.
- Choose solid colors, comfortable and loose clothes, and items that don't require much ironing.
- Choose clothes that are easy to wear, like buttonless or zipper-less pieces and slip-on shoes.
- Ensure their clothes are suitable for the temperature.[111]

Hallucinations

Dementia patients can have hallucinations, especially if they have dementia with Lewy bodies. Visual hallucinations can be simple (seeing flashing lights) or complex (seeing animals or situations). Hallucinations can result from brain damage, physical illness like fever, seizure, stroke, migraine, infection, inflammation, or even side effects of medications. Some people can also hear, smell, feel, or taste things that aren't there.

If your loved one begins to hallucinate:

- Seek medical attention immediately. Hallucinations could indicate an emergency.
- Calmly explain to the patient what is happening.
- Stay with them and ask them to describe the hallucination. Remember not to argue with them while not validating their hallucinations.

---

[111] "Dressing," Dementia Australia, n.d., https://www.dementia.org.au/support-and-services/families-and-friends/personal-care/dressing.

- Try to gently lead them away from where the hallucination is happening. This can end the hallucination.

- Ensure the patient isn't hungry, thirsty, or uncomfortable, as any of these factors can lead to hallucinations.

- See if distracting the patient can stop the hallucination.[112]

Sexual Behavior

Dementia changes everything, and sexuality is not exempt. The patient's needs and desires may change. If the caregiver is also the patient's partner, these changes will have double the effect. However, many partners still enjoy intimacy, and they find new ways to share intimacy after a diagnosis. The changes in the partner may be due to the physical and emotional changes that come with the disease. Some types of dementia, most specifically Frontotemporal Dementia, can affect inhibitions, causing the patient to become more direct and explicit about their sexual interests.

Remember:

- Differences in sexual desire can be expected for any couple, whether they're dealing with dementia or not. It helps to seek practical solutions and talk to a professional if necessary.

- Physical activity or masturbation can release pent-up sexual tension.

- Sex isn't the only form of intimacy. Closeness, massage therapy, or even non-sexual friendships can meet the need for intimacy.

- Support groups are a safe place to express your thoughts and frustrations.[113]

---

[112] "Hallucinations and Dementia," Alzheimer's Society, February 26, 2021, https://www.alzheimers.org.uk/about-dementia/symptoms-and-diagnosis/hallucinations.
[113] "How Does Dementia Affect Sex and Intimacy?," Alzheimer's Society, n.d., https://www.alzheimers.org.uk/get-support/daily-living/sex-intimacy-dementia#content-start.

Verbal Outbursts

As we discussed before, dementia can cause patients to act in ways that are verbally and physically aggressive. Of course, this is distressing for the patient, caregiver, and anyone else who may witness such aggression. Verbal outbursts may include swearing, screaming, shouting, or threats. Remember that the brain is undergoing significant changes, which is the cause of this behavior. Patients may have outbursts due to memory loss, language problems, mental or physical health issues, too much or too little contact with people, distressing physical surroundings, frustration, confusion, or a feeling of being out of control. These symptoms can present whether or not the person was already aggressive before dementia.

If this outburst behavior appears:

- Find out if the patient is in physical pain or mental distress. Alleviating these things can help with outbursts.

- Do your best to maintain a daily routine.

- Support the patient in staying as independent as possible for as long as possible.

- Help the patient to stay in contact with their family and friends so they don't feel isolated.

- Support the patient in participating in activities they enjoy.[114]

If your loved one is in the middle of an outburst, here are some strategies to try in the moment:

- As difficult as it may be, try to stay calm. An angry response can make things worse. Take a deep breath, and don't feel compelled to respond immediately. Give yourself and your loved one some time.

---

[114] "Aggressive Behaviour and Dementia," Alzheimer's Society, December 13, 2021, https://www.alzheimers.org.uk/about-dementia/symptoms-and-diagnosis/symptoms/aggressive-behaviour-and-dementia.

- Give yourself and your loved one some space. If appropriate, step out of the room for a while.

- Do not shout, move too close to the person, or initiate physical contact, as these actions may be perceived as a threat.

- Avoid body language that seems closed off, like crossing your arms. Instead, mirror their body language. Sit if they're sitting. Stand if they're standing. Place your hands in your lap if that's what they're doing. This signals that you are not against them, and you want to help.

- Listen to them, maintain eye contact, and explain why you're there.

- If things become physical, leave and find help..[115]

Shadowing

Shadowing is when a dementia patient follows their caregiver around. They may mimic the caregiver, walk everywhere they go, and become anxious if the caregiver is ever away. This behavior appears to be driven by anxiety and uncertainty. To the patient, the caregiver feels like the only certain thing, so when they leave, even to go to the bathroom, the patient becomes upset. This can make the caregiver feel smothered and annoyed. To find relief, try a few of these coping mechanisms:

- Remind yourself that your loved one is afraid and anxious instead of feeling like they're just trying to irritate you. Perception has the power to change your response.

- To be a good caregiver, you need a break every now and then. Do your best to find some quiet time. It can be in the shower, when the patient is asleep, or even during an allotted time in the routine where you set the alarm and assure them you'll return to the room when the timer goes off.

---

[115] "Aggressive Behaviour and Dementia."

- Try to recruit someone else, like a neighbor, friend, or family member to spend time with the patient so you can get a break.

- Try to reduce shadowing by involving your loved one in meaningful, engaging activities like gardening or completing a puzzle.

- Give the patient a snack or gum to distract them.

- Music benefits dementia patients, so give them headphones to listen to their favorite songs. You can also offer them a recording of your voice for added comfort.[116]

After Sheila's wandering incident, she started shadowing Kendra. Kendra figured that the aftermath of the incident—the sight of the police car, all the people watching, and the realization that she wasn't where she was supposed to be—all scared Sheila. Also, Sheila must have realized that she wouldn't get lost again if she never left Kendra's side. Kendra's recognition of this anxiety helped her to cope with Sheila's shadowing. It was difficult, as she started to feel like she could never get a moment to herself, but she had more patience for the shadowing because she understood where it was coming from. This was also the edge Kendra needed to call Sheila's friend, Meredith, and ask her to come over a few times a week to keep Sheila company. These became built-in times for Kendra to take a break and take a breath.

This is a lot to think about, and it's even more to deal with once the dementia behaviors appear. As hard as it may be, try to keep top of mind how hard it must be for your loved one to live out these experiences without even fully understanding what's happening to or around them. While these behaviors are frustrating for you, they're not malicious; they usually have a reason behind them. Think about what you know to be true about the patient's personality and life before dementia to help filter the meanings behind their actions. For example, if they worked the night shift during their working years, that could explain why they prefer to stay up at night. They may be trying to feel like their

---

[116] Esther Heerema Msw, "Shadowing in Alzheimer'S Disease," Verywell Health, February 10, 2023, https://www.verywellhealth.com/shadowing-in-alzheimers-97620.

old selves. And remember not to argue. If a conversation contains incorrect information, redirect your loved one, instead.[117]

Other ways to manage these changing behaviors are to spend quality time over tea or games with the patient; call or video chat them if you're away; think about how you can support their emotions; and use former coping mechanisms, like keeping a consistent schedule, reminiscing, or going for regular walks to burn off excess energy as cues on how to handle things now.

In former medicinal practices, doctors regularly prescribed antipsychotic drugs to dementia patients. However, it became clear that most of these drugs had limited to no benefits for those with dementia and carried serious side effects. They should be prescribed as a last resort and only if behaviors persistently cause severe distress or put them or others in harm's way. They should be used alongside other non-drug approaches, and this should always happen under a doctor's supervision.

To wrap up, here is a list of steps to help manage challenging behaviors:

1. **Identify the problem.**
   a. Is the patient's behavior causing a problem?
   b. Is it others' reactions to the behavior that's causing a problem?
   c. Is the patient's environment or living situation causing a problem?
   d. Is there some other factor, like trying to communicate hunger, thirst, pain, boredom, or a different need?

2. **Look at the situation.**
   a. When and where does the behavior take place?

---

[117] "Reducing and Managing Behaviour That Challenges," Alzheimer's Society, August 13, 2021, https://www.alzheimers.org.uk/about-dementia/symptoms-and-diagnosis/symptoms/managing-behaviour-changes.

b. Does it always happen under the same circumstances?

c. Are other people involved? If so, who?

d. Do the patient's questions have a common theme?

e. Are there triggers that cause the behavior?

3. **Consider how the patient is feeling when they exhibit these behaviors.**

    a. Are they tired, overstimulated, or scared?

    b. Are they feeling embarrassed, ignored, misunderstood, or patronized?

    c. Are they depressed or having hallucinations?

    d. Are they bored, under stimulated, or lacking social contact?

    e. Are they physically uncomfortable, like too hot or too cold?

4. **Identify anything the person could be reacting to.**

    a. Are they realizing that there are things they can no longer do?

    b. Did something unpleasant happen?

    c. Did they have a sad memory?

    d. Has someone provoked them?

5. **Develop a strategy.**

    a. Talk to the patient and the people they spend time with and make a plan.

    b. Implement changes one or two at a time to see if they make a difference in behaviors. For example, you could change the way you talk to them or the time of day you handle specific tasks. Most

THE PRACTICAL DEMENTIA CAREGIVER GUIDE

importantly, be consistent. Make sure everybody involved in the care plan uses the same strategies.

6. **Keep a record.**
   a. All the changes won't work, and that's okay.
   b. Keep a record of what works, even if it doesn't work every time.
   c. Share the record with others who spend time around the patient.[118]

You might feel overwhelmed after reading about all the things that can happen, but not all days are bad days. Everything won't happen at once, and you may never even encounter some of these behaviors. Take it one day at a time and take it one hour or minute at a time each day. Staying in the moment and not taking behaviors personally are the keys to caring for a loved one with dementia.

The suggestions here are factors you can control, but there will always be factors you cannot. You can't control what a patient thinks, how a medicine might cause them to react, or how quickly the dementia progresses. However, you can make adjustments based on changes and use trial and error to determine how to handle sticky situations. Most of all, remember to give yourself grace. As long as you are doing your best, you're doing enough.

Hopefully this chapter has made you more aware and equipped for the myriad ways your loved one's behaviors could change over the coming months and years. From bathing to wandering, problems with eating to outbursts, there are things you can do to help them and you feel better. No matter what strategies you try, remember that the patient is feeling emotional about the changes in themselves, too, and your reactions and responses give them cues about how to behave.

---

[118] "Reducing and Managing Behaviour That Challenges."

Take Action

Take a few moments to write down any behaviors mentioned in this chapter that you may have already noticed in the person you care for. Then, make a table with two columns. On the left side, write down the way you handled the situation. On the right side, write down a coping mechanism you learned in this chapter that could be as effective or more effective than what you're currently doing. If any behavior has you stumped, don't hesitate to reach out to your doctor.

In the next chapter, we'll explore the importance of spending meaningful time with your loved one doing things that bring them joy. You'll find that bringing them joy usually means bringing joy to yourself.

CHAPTER 8

Finding Common Ground

I had grown accustomed to the first few minutes of my visits with Sheila and Kendra consisting of an update on the new behaviors Sheila had displayed that made caring for her more difficult. However, one day when I entered the exam room, Kendra was smiling.

"I can't wait to tell you what happened," she said. "A few days ago, we were walking through the neighborhood and passed by the park where we used to play when we were kids. We walked along the path, and there was nobody on the swings. There's always somebody on the swings."

I nodded my head and noticed the serenity on both of the women's faces.

"Sheila asked if I wanted to get on a swing. I started to say no because I feared she might fall, but I decided to go along. I helped Sheila into a swing, and I sat in the one right next to it. She started to pump her legs. She only went back and forth a little bit, but she was smiling and laughing. She told me to swing, too, so I did. Before I knew it, we were both laughing as we swung in those swings like two boulders on a piece of yarn!"

"We get on the swing every day, don't we Kendra?" Sheila asked.

"Yes, we sure do," Kendra responded with a nod.

Kendra went on to tell me how Sheila had taught her how to swing when they were kids and how they would ride their bikes to the park every day in the summer and stay there for hours. This was the first time they had been on a swing in years. Under Kendra's careful supervision, they enjoyed a few minutes remembering simpler times.

Remembering the importance of your role in moments of serenity and joy will help temper the times that may not be so peaceful.

As dementia changes the brain, and those physical changes cause changes in behavior, relationships will change, too. But even though relationships may change, the need for love and affection does not. Sometimes, this need for affection can show up as shows of affection at inappropriate times. The caregiver's role in the relationship is likely to shift. You may become responsible for things you weren't responsible for before, like finances. Your relationship with family and friends might change. They might not feel they know how to behave around the patient or what to say about the situation, so they may avoid you … which means it might fall on you to reach out to them with suggestions about what to say and do around the patient. While it may be tempting to avoid those who avoid you, it's better to reach out to potential sources of support and guide the conversation. The illness itself may cause changes in the behavior of loved ones who either can't accept the disease or don't feel equipped to help out. This can cause resentment, disagreements, and a lack of input in important decisions.

Consider holding a family meeting so you can address everyone simultaneously. Say upfront that everyone may not agree with the decisions that need to be made but be sure to communicate those decisions as you make them so no one feels left out.

Everyone in the patient's life will feel the impact of a dementia diagnosis. The patient will become the center of attention, whether they were before or not. This newly focused attention can cause other family members, like spouses or children, to feel neglected. Feeling neglected can make them feel resentful for not getting the attention they need. People may also feel burdened if they have to take on new responsibilities, like chores or sitting with the patient. These feelings can lead to withdrawal, negativity, and even divorce.

Remember that people can react to the same situation in many different ways, and those reactions can run the gamut from close and helpful to withdrawn and divisive. On the other hand, in some families, dementia brings a newfound sense of closeness as loved ones pull together to work through the situation. In doing so, some people learn they have strengths they didn't know they had. Either way, dementia often comes with a few common, heavy emotions for family and friends.

Guilt

Illness somehow humanizes people in a way that elicits a new level of remorse or responsibility. As a result of a dementia diagnosis, people close to the patient may feel guilty for how they treated the patient sometime in the past, shame or embarrassment due to the patient's new strange behaviors, or guilt for lost tempers or lack of caring for the sick person. Suppose the patient has to go to the hospital or enter a care facility. In that case, caregivers may feel bad for not being able to keep them home longer, even if they've done everything they possibly could to help. If you've made promises like, "I'll always be there for you," you may now feel like you're not upholding those promises.

Grief and Loss

Since we know there is no cure for dementia, a diagnosis means facing the inevitable twofold loss of a loved one. The loss will eventually come through their demise, but there is also the loss of the person you've always known them to be. Grief for the loss of the future you'd imagined together is a normal, healthy response. Like all emotions, everyone will experience these feelings of grief differently.

Anger

Anger is a natural feeling that comes with caring for someone with dementia. It may be anger at the disease itself, anger at having to care for the patient, anger towards those who aren't helping, anger at the difficult patient, or anger at support services. This anger can get overwhelming, and the feelings of distress, frustration, guilt, and exhaustion can make you feel like shaking, pushing, or even hitting the dementia patient. If you ever feel like you may lose control, discussing these feelings with your doctor or someone in a support role is vitally important.

Young Family Members

One group often forgotten while caring for a dementia patient is the young people in the family. Given the demands of dementia care, teens and children may suddenly lose the attention they're used to. Therefore, explaining the disease to them in a way that they understand and allowing them to pitch in is essential.

Children often feel a variety of emotions when a grandparent is diagnosed. They might be scared they did something to cause the dementia, or they might think they can catch it themselves. Teens might become resentful if they are called on to help or feel embarrassed that their grandparent is different. College-age children might feel reluctant to leave the family for school. It's important to reassure children that they can't cause or catch dementia and to be blunt about the changes to come. Let them know the patient will forget things, they may say or do things that make them feel embarrassed, or they may become emotional at unexpected times. Tell them this is all a result of the disease's impact on the brain and nothing else.

The Rouse family had six siblings, all of whom had children of their own. Robert and Tina had 28 grandchildren between their six sons and daughters. The family went on vacations together whenever possible, spending plenty of time at Rob and Tina's home. When Rob's dementia symptoms became too intense to ignore and he was diagnosed with Alzheimer's, the family was concerned about how to tell the little ones, who ranged in age from 3-24. I gave them resources to help explain what was happening to Rob, and I spoke with two of Rob and Tina's children to provide them with pointers on how to address the young children. They split the children into groups based on age and approached the conversation in an age-appropriate way with each group. They encouraged dialogue between the children so they could explain things to each other and ask questions they might have been reluctant to ask the adults.

It's essential to tend to emotional needs and find ways to support the young people in the family. Counseling or support groups for kids are great options. Teachers and other school staff can be a source of relief and encouragement if they know about the situation. This is also an opportunity for a legacy project, where you can have the person with dementia leave messages of love and wisdom for the children in the family while they can.

Partners

The bond with the dementia patient probably has the most significant impact on their partner. Their long history and roles in the relationship must take on new life, and they may not know how to handle it. Couples must keep in mind that while one of them has dementia, dementia doesn't define them. Communication and acceptance are the strongest tools at their disposal. When you realize something is out of your control, focus on what you can control. Do things that bring you joy. Make time for activities that the patient can still participate in. Be intentional about not letting the disease take over every aspect of life. For example, if you've always liked to travel, keep traveling and reminiscing about past travels. If you've always enjoyed the outdoors, take walks or sit at the beach. Find ways to leave dementia behind from time to time, but don't forget to plan ahead by giving the necessary attention to attorneys, financial planners, and family members who need to help prepare for the future..[119]

---

[119] "Understanding How Your Relationship May Change," Alzheimer Society of Canada, n.d., https://alzheimer.ca/en/help-support/i-have-friend-or-family-member-who-lives-dementia/understanding-how-your-relationship.

Quality of Life

When dealing with dementia, it's essential to avoid feeling hopeless and to focus on maintaining a good quality of life for the patient as long as possible. Over the past 20 years, research has supported that quality of life can significantly improve when family members or paid caregivers are involved in the patient's care plan. Consider the basic needs that everyone has for a fulfilling life, then consider that those exact basic physical, social, and psychological needs are magnified for those with dementia, even though the needs may require modification. Physical needs may seem the most obvious, meaning those in other categories may be overlooked. But caregivers should remember that they may not be able to do everything the patient feels is necessary and they, the caregivers, need to be cared for, too. Therefore, it's crucial for the patient to have a support system instead of just a support person.

Basic Needs

Caregivers ensure the patient has nutritious food, hydration, and primary personal and hygienic care. They're also responsible for ensuring the patient receives proper medical care and attends all their scheduled appointments.

Comfort and Pain Management

Dementia patients can't consistently articulate their feelings, so it's up to the caregiver to look for cues and assess the patient's behavior for signs of distress like outbursts, combativeness, resistance to help, and wandering.

Movement

Remember that the loss of mental abilities doesn't necessarily mean the loss of physical skills. People with dementia usually still have the desire for physical activity. If it's lacking, that pent-up energy may manifest in problem behaviors. Supervised walks are great outlets for patients. The walks change their environment, provide movement, and give them company. Walking isn't an activity that requires complex rules or processes, so they don't have to remember much to perform it. Also, it helps expend energy, which could promote better sleep. Remember, never let a dementia patient go for a walk by themselves, and in case of bad weather, see if there are exercise classes available in the community for seniors. Light indoor exercises, like walking (supervised) on a treadmill, yoga, chair yoga, and stretching are great alternatives to walking outside. There are many YouTube channels that teach these skills, making them easily accessible.

Hobbies and Activities

The same mental stimulation that everyone needs is the same stimulation that dementia patients need. They may not be able to participate in the activities they're used to, but there are ways to give them the excitement they seek. One way to go about this is to provide micro versions of their previous life.

Here are a few examples of activities you can encourage your loved one to participate in:

- If the patient was a woodworker, giving them sandpaper to rub onto wood can provide the same joy-inducing sensations as before.
- If they worked in their garden but can't do so anymore, they can work with small plants while sitting at a table in their house.
- Performing household tasks, like folding towels or dusting, can be fulfilling.
- Activities having to do with music, like dancing to a song they enjoy, release endorphins and are sure to bring moments of joy.

Social Interactions

According to research from Utah State University, positive social interactions bring about positive responses in dementia patients. Although the patient may not always know who the person is on the other side of the interaction, they understand social cues, nod, smile, or display other signs of positive engagement after a positive interaction. A caregiver's willingness to participate in a conversation can significantly benefit the patient even if it doesn't make much sense to them. They may need prompting to engage in the discussion, so ask them about their wedding day, where they most enjoyed going on vacation as a child, or if they have any plans for the weekend. As always, the purpose isn't for them to make sense or get the facts right, but for the interaction to bring about feelings of positivity and inclusivity.

Kendra told me about a time when this worked for her. Tension with Sheila was increasing, so she was ready to try something new to soften their interactions. She asked Sheila about what she'd enjoyed most about her career.

"You know what was really fun? When I became president of my engineering company. I was the first woman to be the president there. It was hard, but it was worth it."

Kendra knew this wasn't true, but she decided to keep the conversation going.

"What was the hardest thing about it?" Kendra asked.

"Earning the respect of all those men. At that time, nobody thought a woman could be in any position higher than secretary at a company like that, but I worked my way up and eventually, they all had to respect what I brought to the table."

Kendra let Sheila continue. She was surprised by her sister's imagination, which caused her to smile during the conversation. She was, after all, confabulating—coming up with a false memory without intending to deceive. She believed her story wasn't, in essence, lying. Sheila responded to Kendra's smiles, so Kendra continued asking questions with a positive attitude, and began to smile during the conversation. She quickly realized there was no harm in her sister's stories and adopted this as a regular strategy whenever she sensed Sheila's frustration.

Pleasant Environment

Creating a pleasant environment is a delicate balance. Spaces with little stimulation may be dull to the patient. At the same time, spaces with too much noise or visual stimuli may prove overwhelming. Dementia patients appreciate spaces that are calm and beautiful, as they signal to their brain that they are in a safe and good place. Decorating with soft colors and soft lighting, making sure there is enough daylight, and placing plants around the room are a few ways to help a space feel pleasant and welcoming.

Feeling Loved

Acts of love and kindness like smiling, gentle touch, and positive words are almost always welcomed by dementia patients. Because of the changes in the brain, the patient may be confused about who is actually performing these acts. For example, they may think the person speaking to and hugging them is someone from their life who has already passed on; however, the words and actions make them feel good. What's most important is how the patient feels, as the act itself is still meaningful.

Joy

Dementia patients can still experience happiness. They can feel the energy in a room and respond to it. Small things, like twirling in a circle, may delight them. They are aware when a good time is happening around them. By doing all you can to bring joy through words, actions, positive body language, and gentle touch, you are improving the patient's quality of life despite the inevitable hard times.

Determining Quality of Life

In the early stages of dementia, caregivers can feel assured that their efforts are working by simply asking the patient how they feel. But as the disease progresses and communication becomes more complex, knowing whether you're doing things right can feel like a mystery. At this point, caregivers can determine the patient's quality of life by facial cues and body language, like how often they smile, frown, make eye contact, or look away. As dementia progresses, it will be more of the caregiver's responsibility to initiate activities that bring a sense of calm and care to the patient.[120] A straightforward thing caregivers can do is ensure a bit of social interaction for the patient each day.

New research presented at the Alzheimer's Association International Conference found that ten minutes of interaction each day resulted in an improvement in the well-being of dementia patients. Still, it's been determined that ten minutes is not enough. Experts are advocating for a person-centered approach to care that considers the patient's needs, abilities, interests, and preferences.[121] Until this is the norm, schedule daily interaction with your loved one into the routine as much as possible, face-to-face, or digitally.

With the right surroundings, people with dementia can live satisfying lives for many years after their diagnosis. This means less worrying behavior as well as less stress for caregivers. Here are a few reminders for how to establish safe and pleasant surroundings:

- **Provide a feeling of safety and comfort**

    Make the necessary changes in the home to elicit feelings of safety. If necessary, be more intentional about listening and speaking in soft tones to help reduce the patient's feelings of frustration.

- **Provide an environment of relaxation and emotional support**

    Consider music, aromatherapy, or a sacred space for prayer and quiet time. If the patient finds it relaxing, keep their pet close, or consider a pet if they don't have one. Kendra found it helpful to light a candle for Sheila next to her armchair each morning so she could listen to her favorite preacher's online videos and pray. Starting the day this way

---

[120] Elizabeth B. Fauth, Maria C. Norton, and Jessica J. Weyerman, "Maximizing the Quality of Life for Persons with Dementia," Healthy Aging, accessed March 13, 2024, https://digitalcommons.usu.edu/cgi/viewcontent.cgi?article=2822&context=extension_curall.
[121] "Ten Minutes of Social Interaction Improves Wellbeing in Dementia Care," Alzheimer's Society, July 30, 2018, https://www.alzheimers.org.uk/news/2018-07-30/ten-minutes-social-interaction-improves-wellbeing-dementia-care.

provided a sense of calm and "groundedness" that readied them both for the day.

- **Provide meaningful activities**

    Involve the patient in activities that make them feel useful, like folding laundry, performing safe cooking tasks, dusting, arranging photo albums, or working in the garden. Make sure these activities will make them feel good, not burdened. Make space for mistakes and give the patient adequate time to perform tasks at their own pace. Remember, all their abilities won't falter simultaneously, so show them options that are appropriate for what they can still do. Be sure to involve activities that keep them moving, like walking, so they can release pent-up energy and get the exercise they need.

- **Have fun!**

    Life is not over after a diagnosis of dementia. Patients can still play games, enjoy outings, and interact with other people. Figure out what they like and what is safe and include these activities in their lives. Keep these activities free of pressure, and approach them like everyday activities instead of doctor-mandated ones. If an activity seems like it would be fun to you, but the patient isn't interested, move on to something else.

- **Relax and talk**

    Dementia will bring times of high stress, but every moment won't be stressful. When there is an opportunity to relax, take it. In times of low stress, dementia patients can often remember things of the past, and they'll enjoy sharing these experiences. One thing to do during these times is to look at simple books with illustrations. Caregivers can read along or even act out the scenes in the story. Music can provide a relaxing mood or bring back positive memories. Songs from films or childhood jingles can elicit those memories and provide entertaining conversation. Scents and spices can trigger thoughts of happy times, and reminiscing can provide an opportunity to record the patient's life experiences creatively.

- **Do's and Don'ts**

    Remember to do your best to make the patient feel like an active participant in their own life. Make adjustments so that activities don't seem so easy that they're condescending or so complicated that they're impossible. Let them handle activities at their own pace and choose meaningful things. Do not:

- Force patients to do anything they don't want to do
- Supervise them constantly to make them do things correctly
- Rush them
- Do anything that could put them in danger
- Try to correct their mistakes
- Laugh at them.[122]

Always aim to be kind, empathetic, and understanding. Doing so is easier said than done in moments of difficulty. Dementia is all about moments. Some will be difficult, while others will be sweet. Make it a practice to stay in the moment. Although the patient's memory is fading, what matters most is what is happening "in the now."

Take Action

What relationships have changed as a result of your patient's dementia diagnosis? Write down the changes that have occurred and consider whether there are any conversations you can have that could make communication

---

[122] Dementia Care Notes, "Improve the Quality of Life of Persons With Dementia | Dementia Care Notes," Dementia Care Notes, India, December 8, 2022, https://dementiacarenotes.in/caregivers/quality-of-life/.

easier between you, other caregivers, and the loved ones affected by the diagnosis.

What practices have you established to bring moments of relief and joy to the patient you're caring for? Make a list of what has been most enjoyable, then go back through this chapter and mark 2-3 new practices you can establish to bring forth positive feelings and happy memories.

Next, we will move to the third section of this guide. In the following chapter, we'll focus on your role as a caregiver and how that role will evolve as dementia progresses in the patient. We'll discuss what you should expect from the disease, the expectations you should and should not put on yourself, and ways to care for yourself as you care for your loved one.

PART THREE
ASSESS

CHAPTER 9

Understanding Your Role

Before Sheila's diagnosis, Kendra didn't know what her day-to-day life would look like. She knew things would become hard and that they could become hard quickly, but she was primarily uninformed of the physical, emotional, and financial implications of her sister's illness. Kendra went from being a carefree younger sister to feeling like her sister's life was in her hands. As things became progressively more intense and she began to feel worn down, she questioned her ability to continue caring for her sister. Kendra was exhausted. She had become irritable with people who had nothing to do with the situation, she had lost touch with friends who had been fixtures in her life before her sister's diagnosis, and her exercise routine had become non-existent. These feelings and realities are virtually universal for informal caregivers.

As a reminder, there are two types of caregivers. Formal caregivers are paid to care for patients, either in their homes or in a care facility. When we say "caregiver" in this book, we're referring to informal caregivers, unpaid people who are usually loved ones who assist patients with daily living and medical tasks. Let's look at the numbers again as they apply to unpaid caregivers.

- In 2020, 41.8 million Americans provided unpaid care to an adult over the age of 50.
- 89% of caregivers provide care for a relative or other loved one, such as a spouse.

- Caregivers provide an estimated $470 billion in free labor each year.
- Caregivers provide unpaid care to loved ones for an average of 4.5 years.
- Family caregivers who live with their senior relative spend an average of 37.4 hours a week on direct caregiving duties. Those who don't live with their relatives spend 23.7 hours a week on these duties.[123]

With this data in mind, you might be feeling overwhelmed. Hopefully, it helps you feel less alone, but that doesn't negate the challenges you'll face when it's just you and your loved one dealing with dementia. No two experiences are the same. Your family dynamics, the stage of the disease, the personality of your loved one, and many other variables will determine your entry into the caregiver position, the duration of time you'll be in this position, and the changes in the position that will occur due to the nature of the disease. The trajectory of your role and responsibilities is affected by the needs of the patient and the settings in which this care may be provided.

As a caregiver, you'll play an advocacy role. You'll interact with multiple providers, transition from home to a hospital or a rehabilitation facility, move to an assisted living facility and, ultimately, handle end-of-life care. Each transition will mean a change for you. It will also indicate a change in health and functional status for the patient, which can affect the caregiver's social, physical, and emotional health. A caregiving episode is determined in terms of duration and intensity, meaning the hours spent caregiving each day, week, or month. Intensity will vary with the patient's level of impairment. Those assisting only with household activities spend an average of 85 hours a month providing care, while those who care for a patient with three or more self-care or mobility needs spend 253 hours caring for the patient per month. This time span is almost equal to two full-time jobs.

The caregiver's everyday life intersects with the role and responsibilities in their own lives apart from caregiving in different ways. Ideally, the caregiver can

---

[123] Samuels, "Caregiver Statistics: A Data Portrait of Family Caregiving in 2023," June 15, 2023.

balance their roles, but as caregiving demands accumulate and caregiving costs become overwhelming, other aspects of the caregiver's life may become overshadowed. If family members disagree, the trajectory can also become more complex. Phases in the caregiving trajectory are as follows:

Awareness

The awareness phase includes recognizing the patient's increasing disabilities, changes in health, and behavioral changes that signal the need for caregiving. The patient may downplay their need for care at this phase out of concern for burdening others. Awareness of their condition can happen gradually or suddenly. Many questions accompany this phase as the caregiver tries to determine how to meet the patient's needs. One or more family members typically assume the caregiver role in response to these needs. Existing relationships, gender roles, cultural norms, and geographic proximity usually determine who this person will be.

Unfolding Responsibility

Ambiguity may occur as the caregiver tries to figure out their role. This may mean redefining their relationship with the patient and other people close to the patient. Social changes occur as you shift from your usual activities. The role is unpredictable, which may lead to uncertainty about the future. The caregiver's confidence is linked to the status of the patient's illness coupled with the caregiver's knowledge and skills of the patient's needs.

Increasing Care Demands

The caregiver's initial tasks may involve monitoring symptoms and medications, managing household tasks, communicating with healthcare professionals, and providing emotional support to the patient. Over time, these tasks may include giving self-care tasks, becoming a decision-maker for the care recipient, and providing specialized care, like giving injections. The caregiving trajectory becomes more complex and intense as dementia progresses to the middle and late stages.

End of Life

This phase may involve nursing home care and repeated hospitalizations as the patient's health declines. This means the caregiver will likely be involved in end-of-life caregiving, like palliative or supportive care. As demands become more urgent and intensive, caregivers may experience increased burden and stress. However, they may also find greater meaning in caregiving at the end of life.

Roles of Family Caregivers

The responsibility of the family caregiver can range from assisting with daily activities and providing direct care to the patient to navigating complex healthcare and social service systems. These responsibilities may include household tasks, hygienic tasks, mobility, emotional and social support, health and medical care, advocacy, care coordination, and surrogacy. Each of these categories has multiple tasks attached. Each domain demands continual problem-solving, decision-making, and communication with healthcare professionals and family members. At the same time, the caregiver must still be vigilant about the patient's well-being. A caregiver's responsibilities may include:

Assisting with Household Tasks, Self-Care, Mobility, and Supervision

It's common for caregivers to assist with shopping, housework, meals, bills, money management, and home maintenance. These activities are often daily responsibilities. Forty-four percent of caregivers report helping with these activities every day or most days. Almost 18% of caregivers help with self-care tasks like bathing, dressing, feeding, and toileting every day or most days. It is common for caregivers of dementia patients to assist with these tasks on a daily basis.

Providing Emotional and Social Support

The emotional and social support older adults need after a difficult diagnosis is different from what they usually receive from family and friends. As their needs increase, they may not be able to reciprocate the caregiver's efforts the way they could before. Additionally, the patient's emotional responses to changing circumstances may require more support from the caregiver. As a result, the caregiver may experience symptoms of depression, anxiety, irritability, or anger. These changes may not be noticeable at first. In fact, the caregiver may not notice changes in the relationship until they've been present for a while.

Health and Medical Care

Family involvement in healthcare has become much more common than in the past. Caregivers are performing tasks in the home that used to be reserved for healthcare professionals in healthcare settings. This is partially because of the efforts to reduce patients' time in long-term care facilities and hospitals, plus the increasing complexity of figuring out the best placement for patients with chronic and acute conditions. Today, more complex medical care can be provided at home compared to the past. For example, in addition to simple oral medication, caregivers can give different forms of injections to the patients at home. Caregivers may also manage drains, tubes, catheters, and tracheostomies while managing symptoms and monitoring the patient's condition.

"I'm not a nurse," Kendra said to me at one of Sheila's appointments when I asked her about Sheila's medications. "I'm having a hard time keeping up with all of this. I can't even pronounce most of these names."

As Sheila's health deteriorated, she began to bump into things and fall more often. Kendra was doing her best but felt it wasn't enough. Sheila had gotten up in the middle of the night one night, fallen, and cut her arm. First, Kendra blamed herself. She thought she had thoroughly accident-proofed the home to prevent injuries, yet it seemed her efforts were not as effective as she had hoped. Then, she felt overwhelmed by having to tend to the stitches on Sheila's arm. Around the same time, we started Sheila on subcutaneous insulin injections that Kendra needed to administer every day. When I asked how things were going, I could feel her exhaustion and frustration. I reminded her of the array of educational programs and resources available to her. You can use the resource finder on the **Alzheimer's Association website** to see if your community offers classes like this. If not, there are online courses available for free.

Scan the QR codes below to access the Alzheimer's Association resources.

https://www.alz.org/

https://training.alz.org/

Advocacy and Care Coordination

The caregiver's role as an advocate is to identify the patient's needs and help them obtain necessary healthcare resources. This might mean determining the patient's eligibility for services and the costs of those services. Healthcare providers, public and private community-based agencies, employers, and payers (Medicare, Medicaid, and private gap insurance plans) can be confusing, and caregivers often must navigate these challenges with no assistance. There are added layers of difficulty if the patient or caregiver is LGBT, faced with limited English language or literacy, or is part of a racial or ethnic group in which standard care is not tailored to their specific needs. Even if the patient moves into a care facility, the family caregiver is often still involved in similar tasks.

You can advocate for your loved one by:

- Clearly communicating their needs and vulnerabilities to formal caregivers
- Asking important questions and sharing critical facts with medical professionals
- Being tenacious about their needs being met
- Ensuring medical staff have your contact information and ask them for frequent updates
- Keeping records updated so you can readily provide documentation when necessary.[124]

My patient, Freddie, was sure that he'd finalized a gap insurance policy while he was still employed that would be in force throughout his retirement. When expensive bills for his care kept showing up in the mail and bill collectors started calling every hour, he was upset, as was his daughter, Gloria. Gloria figured that in his condition, her father thought he'd finalized that policy but hadn't actually gone through with it. Her father insisted, so despite her misgivings, Gloria went to work to prove him right.

Gloria gathered all the paperwork she thought she'd need to prove that Freddie's insurance policy would cover his dementia care. She called the 1-800 numbers on the paperwork, asked her father questions, listened patiently as he struggled with the answers, and found the problem: someone who worked for the insurance company hadn't finished inputting the information in the system,

---

[124] Constance Schein RN, "8 Steps to Advocate for Your Loved One Living With Dementia | Aegis Living," Aegis Living, February 2, 2024, https://www.aegisliving.com/resource-center/advocate-for-your-loved-one-with-dementia/#:~:text=You%20can%20communicate%20their%20vulnerabilities,their%20needs%20are%20being%20met.

even though the approval notice was written in the notes. It turned out Freddie was right and immediately, thousands of dollars in financial frustration were erased. Advocacy takes time and patience, but the payoff almost always outweighs the work.

Decision Making and Surrogacy

Caregivers often fall into the role of decision-maker concerning advance directives, advisory, and even end-of-life support, especially if the care recipient has limited cognitive abilities. Even if patients can express their desires, they may lack the cognition to carry them out. This leaves the caregiver to confront decisions about treatment choices, location of care, and end-of-life care. Considerations for these decisions include preferences, needs, goals, abilities, perceptions, religion, family dynamics, finances, and practicality. The patient and caregiver may not agree on all these elements. While it's still possible, the caregiver should learn all they can from the patient about their preferences to respect their wishes, as the patient's opinion is primary. The patient and family need to decide who will be responsible for these decisions so they can equip themselves with the necessary tools to carry out the patient's desires when the time comes.

Advance directives are legal documents that give instructions for a patient's medical care once they cannot communicate their own wishes. The two most common types are a living will and a power of attorney for healthcare. All it takes is signed paperwork to put these directives into effect. You can request these forms from your doctor or find them online through websites like the AARP site that provides the correct forms by state.

Scan the QR code below to access the AARP Advance Directive Forms.

https://www.aarp.org/caregiving/financial-legal/free-printable-advance-directives/

Preparedness of Caregiving

The caregiver role is varied and complex, involving specialized knowledge, flexibility, and communication skills. However, evidence suggests that many caregivers are not adequately prepared for their responsibilities. A 2015 National Alliance for Caregiving and AARP Public Policy Institute survey found that half of the caregivers of adults 50 and older with dementia reported having to provide medical tasks with no prior preparation. Many caregivers said they learned by trial and error and were afraid of making mistakes. Responsibilities are broad in scope and require a significant time commitment. Unfortunately, caregiver education has not yet been systemically addressed, and training for those in the role is inconsistent. However, reading this book is a major step in providing the education and preparation you'll need for the dementia journey ahead. Additionally, websites, YouTube, other social media, and support groups can help fill the gaps of knowledge you may encounter in the process.

The Impact of Caregiving

The impact caregiving has on the caregiver depends on many variables. There is a risk for adverse effects on the caregivers' well-being in almost every aspect of their lives, ranging from their health to relationships and economic security. There can also be positive effects, like a sense of confidence in their abilities and closeness with the care recipient. There's also the confidence that the patient is being cared for well. Let's look at the effects of the role more closely.

Psychological Effects

Although the psychological effects of caregiving can be positive or negative, the negatives usually outweigh the positives. It's important to recognize and honor the psychological effects caregiving has on you and seek help when necessary.

Negative Psychological Aspects

Adverse effects of caregiving can range from feelings of frustration and stress to symptoms of depression and anxiety. Experts report a higher rate of psychological distress among caregivers than those who are not caregivers, with especially high rates of depression in those caring for patients with dementia. The more hands-on care family caregivers provide, the greater their distress. However, the symptoms persist even after the patient is moved to a long-term care facility. The causes of this lingering distress include worrying about adequate care in the facility, lack of communication with the care facility's staff and physicians, the challenges of surrogate decision-making, and lack of support in care planning and end-of-life decisions. Research shows that psychological effects are most evident in transitional periods of the care cycle, such as when care begins, when the patient suddenly deteriorates, and when care ends. However, caregiving over a long period can have cumulative effects. It appears that those who served the role for five years showed more symptoms than those who did so over two years, even when compared to caregivers whose care recipients had died.

Positive Psychological Aspects

Yes, caregiving can be a tremendous challenge, but many in the role find the experience rewarding. They find a refreshed appreciation of life, personal growth, confidence in their self-control, mastery of new skills, higher self-esteem, and closer relationships. The positive effects may cancel out some of the negative impacts of caregiving, as feelings of positivity make the burden feel lighter, a win for overall mental health.

Xander was young and had a family of his own. His children were involved in orchestra, debate, and soccer, which meant he didn't have a lot of extra time to spare. When his mother, Lily, was diagnosed with dementia, his entire world was rearranged. His wife was supportive and willing to make the necessary adjustments for Xander to spend as much time with his mother as he could. However, Xander wasn't interested in turning his life upside-down. He knew that it would come to this someday since he was an only child, but he didn't expect it to be so early, and he certainly didn't expect it to be by way of dementia. During his mother's visits, he'd give one-word responses to any questions I had and spend the time messaging on his phone.

Xander and Lily came into my office on a particularly busy day. When I walked into the room, the first question Xander asked was, "Why are there so many people out there by themselves?"

"What do you mean?" I asked.

"There are a lot of people who look my mom's age and older out there by themselves. Who's with them?" he asked.

"Oh. You'd be surprised at how many patients have to deal with this alone," I responded.

He furrowed his eyebrows and looked at his mother.

"Do they drive themselves?"

"Some of them do, yes. Some of them get dropped off and picked back up. Some of them go home alone. Lily is lucky to have you," I said. "The days aren't just difficult for caregivers, they're even more difficult for patients. Honestly, no one should have to endure this with anything other than a lot of love and support."

After that day, Xander's attitude did a 180. He began treating Lily with care, holding her hand walking in and out of the office, and fully engaging in our conversations about the progress of her dementia and what he'd need to do next. He started researching more about his mother's condition on his own and asking questions, and he went out of his way to make her comfortable. He contacted me after his mother died and told me how that time ended up teaching him more about love than he'd ever learned before, and even though the situation got worse, his attitude made the difference between what could have been the worst time in his life and what turned out to be the most valuable time in his life.

Physical Health Effects

Caregiving is in no way a passive activity. The physical and emotional aspects of the work have a combined effect on the caregiver's physical well-being. Let's explore caregiving's consequences on the provider's well-being.

Studies have shown that caregivers report their health as poorer than a non-caregiver's. Their physical health is associated with the burden of the work they provide, the hours of care they provide, the number of caregiving tasks they perform, their time in the role, and the impairments of the care recipient. The Health and Retirement Study found that being a spousal caregiver is a predictor of cardiovascular disease. Longer-term caregivers have twice the risk of short-term caregivers. The same study showed that caregivers of those with dementia are significantly more likely to suffer unintentional weight loss, exhaustion, weakness, and the effects of low physical activity over time. A consistent theme in literature on caregiver health effects is that there is a 63% increased risk of mortality among older spousal caregivers if they also reported emotional strain in the caregiving role. Conversely, several recent studies show caregiving to be associated with lower mortality risk. These studies may find a middle ground if we consider that the negative studies are typically based on older, strained caregiving spouses who provide intense levels of care. In contrast, the positive studies focus on all caregivers, regardless of age or relationship to the patient.

Caregiving-Related Injuries

Providing care to an older adult is a physically taxing responsibility involving transfers, lifts, bathing, dressing, and patient positioning. These activities can lead to backaches, muscle strains, and bruises. These injuries are more magnified in older caregivers who may have poor balance, issues with arthritis, or age-related changes in muscle mass. The home environment can contribute to the risk of injury if spaces are too small to perform necessary tasks adequately, rooms are too cluttered, or stairs are too steep.

Physical limitations contributed to Kendra's frustration when Sheila cut her arm. Kendra was in her sixties and had difficulty lifting, transferring, and balancing Sheila several times a day. Things were manageable when Sheila had more mobility. Now, Kendra was starting to feel like she was putting them both in danger, and once the cut happened, she was afraid of what might happen next.

Physiological Measures

Imbalances in hormones and cell function can contribute to the adverse effects of caring for a patient with dementia. Cortisol (the body's primary stress hormone), adrenaline (fight-or-flight hormone), the immune system, antibodies, insulin, and other elements that contribute to healthy function can all suffer under the weight of dementia caregiving. Studies have also found an increase in cardiovascular stress as well as accelerated aging of the immune system as a result of the burden that accompanies caring for a sick loved one.

The National Library of Medicine breaks down how caregiving has all the components of a chronic stress experience:

Caregiving creates physical and psychological strain over extended periods, is accompanied by high levels of unpredictability and uncontrollability, can create secondary stress in multiple life domains such as work and family relationships, and frequently requires high levels of vigilance. Caregiving fits the formula for chronic stress so well that it is used as a model for studying the health effects of chronic stress.[125]

Health Behaviors

If caregivers fail to take time for their own health, stress may worsen any pre-existing illnesses or make them more vulnerable to new health issues. Take adequate rest, maintain a healthy diet, exercise, take breaks, stay up to date with preventative care, and join support groups. Avoid substance abuse, poor diet, or sedentary behaviors. This may be easier said than done, as caregiving schedules can be unpredictable and time-consuming, there may be little to no help, or the stress of the situation may trigger risky behaviors. In one study of dementia caregivers, nearly one-third of subjects regularly missed their own medication doses, and almost half didn't keep their own healthcare appointments. In a review of 23 studies, caregivers reported riskier health behaviors than non-caregivers. These behaviors are closely correlated with sleep disturbance. Caregivers of dementia patients have more sleep problems than non-caregivers, including waking up throughout the night and trouble falling asleep. Fortunately, the more capable caregivers feel about managing difficulties, the more positive their behaviors are. The higher the ability of the caregiver to control their thoughts and find moments of relief, the fewer negative health risk behaviors they experience, meaning the stress on their well-being is reduced.

Social Effects and Family Relationships

Caregiving can bring changes in family dynamics and social activities. There may be less time to maintain social relationships, and in some instances, caregivers may experience extreme life-changing effects that change relationships even after the disease has run its course. These may include infidelity, spousal abuse, or divorce. The time demands of caregiving often

---

[125] "Positive Aspects of Caregiving." American Psychological Association, 2011. https://www.apa.org/pi/about/publications/caregivers/faq/positive-aspects.

limit opportunities to engage in enjoyable activities, limiting the time the caregiver has for themself.

One study found that the psychological effects of caregiving are not limited to the primary caregiver. Instead, they permeate throughout the family. It found that caregivers of parents with dementia were less happy in their marriages than those not serving as caregivers. Care decisions can bring about family conflict via discussions about boundaries, disapproval of family members' actions or attitudes, disagreements about the nature or seriousness of the patient's condition, failure to appreciate the efforts of the primary caregiver, failure to provide support, disapproval of the quality of care, and disagreements over finances. Sometimes, these disagreements can become so intense that they result in legal action or severed relationships.[126]

The Other Side of the Coin

Without a doubt, these notions could be discouraging, but keep in mind, these are all possible situations, not guaranteed ones. A National Opinion Research Center survey found that 83% of caregivers rate their experience as positive. They feel good about giving back to someone who has cared for them, and they feel confident and satisfied that the patient is receiving quality care. They also find personal growth through the experience, and some of them feel that through their example, things will come full circle, and their own children will care for them when the time comes. Those who find benefits in their caregiving role also suffer from lower levels of depression.[127]

Whether you find yourself amid many of the challenges above simultaneously, or you find caregiving fulfilling, it is paramount to take care of yourself. Failing to do so will have negative implications in every area of your life—physical,

---

[126] Richard Schulz, Jill Eden, and Committee on Family Caregiving for Older Adults, "Family Caregiving Roles and Impacts," Families Caring for an Aging America - NCBI Bookshelf, November 8, 2016, https://www.ncbi.nlm.nih.gov/books/NBK396398/.
[127] "Positive Aspects of Caregiving," *Https://Www.Apa.Org*, n.d., https://www.apa.org/pi/about/publications/caregivers/faq/positive-aspects.

mental, spiritual, and emotional. If you don't take time for yourself to find moments of care and joy, everyone around you will suffer along with you.

It is a regular occurrence for caregivers to end up sick without even realizing it. Please know there is nothing noble about ignoring your own needs and nothing selfish about tending to them. Set goals for yourself concerning your own care, like working out three times a week or meeting up with a friend once a week. Seek solutions instead of reasons why you should put your own needs last. Communicate with other caregivers, health professionals, and family members so everyone is clear about their roles; you can't do everything, and you don't need to try to. Ask for help and accept the help others are willing to give.[128]

Take Action

Take a few minutes to reflect on your caregiving experience so far. Think about the responsibilities you've had to take on in this journey. In which areas could you use more help? Take note so you can seek assistance from willing family and friends, community organizations, or your healthcare provider. Find support groups in your community that cater to your demographic. Has the patient's dementia impacted your relationship with the patient or other relationships in the family? Can you or anyone else do anything to minimize any negative impact? Exploring the answers to these questions is a form of self-care.

In the next chapter, we'll explore overwork, burnout, and the damage each can cause. You'll find strategies to help manage your time, emotions, financial strain, and sleep deprivation. You'll also discover practical ways to put yourself first and leave guilt behind.

---

[128] "Taking Care of YOU: Self-Care for Family Caregivers - Family Caregiver Alliance," Family Caregiver Alliance, January 11, 2023, https://www.caregiver.org/resource/taking-care-you-self-care-family-caregivers/.

CHAPTER 10

Taking Care of Yourself

"Kendra, when was the last time you took some time for yourself?" I asked. Kendra rolled her eyes.

"Are you kidding me?" she asked. I didn't laugh.

"Listen, I don't have time for myself. I barely have time to do everything I need to do for Sheila, especially now since she keeps falling and hurting herself. Time for myself? Please ..."

"When will Tyler be home for another break?" I asked.

"In a few weeks, but he's young. This isn't his responsibility," she answered.

"Didn't he say repeatedly that he wants to help when he's around? Do you not believe him?" I asked.

"He's saying that because he thinks it's what he's supposed to say. Like I said, he's young. Where are all these adults claiming they love Sheila and me but who never come around to help? Where are they?" Kendra asked with tears in her eyes.

"Have you called them and asked them for their help?" I responded.

Kendra was quiet. The tears streamed down her face.

"I have to do this. I'm her sister. Everybody else shouldn't have to put their lives on hold for her like I have. One person giving up everything is enough!"

"If you invited more people in, you wouldn't have to give up everything," I responded. She was sobbing, so I gave her space to do so. She was fed up.

Burnout may be on the horizon when you start to feel like you just can't do it anymore. Caregiver burnout is physical, emotional, and mental exhaustion that can occur when you give your time and energy to manage the health and safety of someone else. Symptoms of burnout include feelings of tiredness that can't be cured by a nap or a day off, stress, withdrawal from social settings, anxiety, and depression. Burnout can impact a person physically, psychologically, financially, and socially. This happens when you've given a disproportionate amount of energy and dedication to someone or something other than yourself, or when you try to do more than you're capable or equipped to do emotionally, physically, or financially.

Caregiver burnout is common. In fact, more than 60% of caregivers experience its symptoms. However, just because something is common doesn't make it acceptable or unworthy of attention.

What are burnout symptoms?

Caregiver burnout looks a lot like anxiety and depression. Symptoms include:

- Emotional and physical exhaustion
- Withdrawal from family, friends, and other loved ones
- Loss of interest in activities you usually enjoy
- Feelings of hopelessness and helplessness
- Changes in appetite and weight
- Changes in sleep patterns
- Inability to concentrate

- Sickness

- Feelings of irritability, frustration, or anger towards others

The role of a caregiver can undoubtedly be overwhelming. These feelings are real, they are valid, and they warrant your attention.

What does caregiver burnout feel like?

Burnout won't feel the same for all caregivers, but common feelings are associated with it. Some of these feelings include:

- Anxiety or fear that if you do something wrong, the person in your care will suffer because of it

- Anger or frustration that the person in your care isn't responding positively to the care you're providing

- Denial of the patient's actual condition

- Guilt for taking time to care for yourself

- Negativity as the patient's illness continues. This can also present as no longer caring whether you do your job well.

- Seclusion or loneliness if you lack support or feel that asking for help is a sign of weakness.

What causes caregiver burnout?

When your energy has been dedicated to caring for someone else, it's easy to put your needs aside. While this exchange of attention might make sense at first and even seem noble, it has a cost. When you neglect yourself, you put your own emotional and mental health at risk, which impacts the way you feel about your ability to carry on your responsibilities to your loved one. This and other factors can contribute to caregiver burnout:

- **Role confusion:** Becoming a caregiver can happen overnight, which makes it a confusing experience. Drawing a line between your role as a caregiver and your role as a child, spouse, sibling, or friend is challenging. As your role emerges, there can be a lack of clarity for you and other family members who are helping, which can be stressful for everyone.

- **Varied expectations:** In the beginning, many caregivers feel that their involvement in the patient's care will be a good thing, but the reality is that caregiving is no easy task. Yes, it can be rewarding, but it's also a challenge. The space between expectation and reality can be hard to reconcile and balance.

- **Lack of control:** While there are things you can control, there are many things that you can't. Those factors may include a lack of finances, resources, or skills that would go a long way in helping to plan, manage, and organize the patient's care.

- **Too many responsibilities:** As you've likely gathered from the information in previous chapters, caregiving is a big puzzle with lots of small pieces. If you're the sole caregiver, all those pieces are yours to align. If you're not the sole caregiver, sometimes you may put more on yourself than is necessary.

- **Not realizing burnout is taking place:** Most people don't even realize they're burning out while it's happening, so they try to keep pushing forward as usual. This impacts the quality of care the caregiver can provide.

This is where Kendra found herself. In the daily grind of schedules, appointments, medications, outbursts, caring for her sister's hygiene, trying to keep her safe, and never knowing what new and frightening thing she would wake up to on any given morning, Kendra didn't realize she was at her wit's end. She hardly reached out to anyone to talk about her feelings because of her guilt. Instead, she kept it all in and pushed through the minutes. She didn't realize how deeply she was hurting herself by handling things like she was doing.

What are the risk factors for caregiver burnout?

You may be at risk of caregiver burnout if you:

- Don't have someone to relieve you when you're tired
- Feel like you're the only one who can do your job successfully

What is the long-term impact of caregiver burnout?

Caregiver burnout is not a short-lived feeling of tiredness that an afternoon of relaxation can heal. It becomes deeply seeded and can affect your ability to care for the patient and yourself. The longer you're in a caregiving role, the more of a risk you have of dealing with burnout, which makes you more vulnerable to physical and mental health conditions. Over time, you might find yourself delaying preventative care or even necessary treatment for a condition you're suffering from. Additionally, if you leave mental health symptoms unchecked, quality of life will plummet for yourself and everyone around you. In severe cases, stress and depression in caregivers can become life-threatening.

How can you prevent caregiver burnout?

One effective strategy is to open up about your experiences and feelings with someone you trust, whether it's a friend, family member, therapist, or support group. Expressing what you're going through can alleviate stress and provide you with emotional support. It's also important to accept your feelings—acknowledge that it's normal to feel overwhelmed or frustrated at times. By setting realistic goals for your caregiving role and educating yourself about your loved one's illness, you can manage expectations and better prepare for the challenges ahead.

Additionally, recognizing your limitations is key to avoiding burnout. Understand that it's okay to ask for help and delegate tasks when necessary. Prioritize self-care by ensuring you get adequate rest, engage in physical activity, and maintain a nutritious diet. These practices are not just vital for your health but also enhance your capacity to care for your loved one. Taking regular breaks, pursuing hobbies, and maintaining social connections can also significantly reduce the risk of burnout, keeping you mentally and physically refreshed and more resilient in your caregiving journey.

How do you recover from caregiver burnout?

The first step to recovering from caregiver burnout is recognizing you have it. After that, it's time to learn how to manage or treat it. There's not one solution to handling it, but there are strategies you can use to feel better:

- Talk to a healthcare provider, like a counselor or psychologist.
- Make time for self-care. Don't skip your own healthcare appointments.
- Be sure to exercise and regularly do things that make you feel good.
- Ask for help in your caregiving responsibilities.
- Find local resources that can be helpful, like food delivery services, community centers, or in-home care for the patient.
- Consider respite care, a temporary break for primary caregivers. Respite care can last from a few hours to a few weeks and can occur in the patient's home or a care facility. Go to ARCH National Respite Network and Resource Center to see what resources are available near you.

Scan the QR code below to access the
National Respite Locator Service.

https://arch.gnosishosting.net/Portal/Registry

How long does it take to get over caregiver burnout?

Once you know you're dealing with burnout and decide to seek help, you can start feeling better in a matter of days, or it could be months before you feel better again. Every situation is different. Just know the sooner you take care of yourself, the sooner you'll feel better, but you didn't start to feel bad overnight, so you won't get better overnight. Give yourself time.

Compassion Fatigue

There is something that resembles caregiver burnout called compassion fatigue. Caregiver burnout is a feeling of profound exhaustion and stress from caring for another person. Compassion fatigue happens when a caregiver takes on the emotional stress and trauma of a person within their care, which results in a lack of empathy or care for the patient. Both voids can happen at the same time and can both impact the caregiver. Be on the lookout for compassion fatigue on top of burnout.[129]

---

[129] Cleveland Clinic Medical Professional, "Caregiver Burnout," Cleveland Clinic, n.d., https://my.clevelandclinic.org/health/diseases/9225-caregiver-burnout.

The Challenges of Being a Caregiver

Being a family caregiver can be a beautiful, rewarding, and fulfilling experience, but it doesn't come without difficulties. There are parts of the experience you may not anticipate. Some of these struggles are as follows:

- **Time management:** Caregivers may have less time for themselves and other family members and responsibilities they'd grown used to. The time they spend caregiving might mean sacrificing time for other things, like hobbies or vacations. Balancing schedules around caregiving can be tricky and inconsistent.

- **Emotional and physical stress:** 22% of caregivers report that their own health has declined as a result of caregiving. Chronic conditions, like dementia, cause the most stress. The physical demands of caregiving can also take a toll.

- **Lack of privacy:** One challenge that may not come to mind until it's reality is the lack of privacy caregivers feel in the home if a loved one comes to live with them, especially if they live in a small space. It can be hard to set boundaries to avoid constant interaction.

- **Financial strain:** Since most caregivers are not paid, finances can get tight, especially if the caregiver has to leave their job to offer help. The longer the caregiver provides care, the more financial strain they feel.

- **Sleep deprivation:** Lack of sleep can cause a snowball of other problems. It can quickly make the caregiver feel like they're burning the candle at both ends.

- **Depression and isolation:** Family caregivers are at risk of depression for several reasons, one of which is that their duties take up so much time that they're no longer able to maintain social connections outside of the home.[130]

Many caregivers don't ask for help because they feel ashamed of sharing the burden with someone else. They may also feel like asking for help is a sign of weakness. As a result, the caregiver starts to feel guilty, which interferes with their ability to care for the patient as well as they would be able to otherwise.

Political efforts are underway to help alleviate some of the financial and emotional strain caregiving can cause. The Lifespan Respite Care Program Reauthorization Act of 2020, which became law in 2021, allows states to implement coordinated respite care programs and provide resources to caregivers on how to gain access to services in their communities. Since 2009, most states have used funding to provide different resources to caregivers. North Carolina, for example, provides $500 in respite care reimbursement to unpaid caregivers, prioritizing those with high financial need. Corrie, a caregiver whom the United States of Care (unitedstatesofcare.org) interviewed, states that when you're a caregiver, "Your brain is functioning for two people all the time," a vivid picture of the strain caregivers deal with to care for their loved ones.[131]

Dealing with Guilt

Kendra felt this pressure of functioning for two people and felt like her life had ended as she knew it. At one point, Sheila got the flu and was in bed for a week. When that happened, Kendra felt a sense of freedom. She felt less guilty about asking a home health aide to come over and sit with Sheila while she was out for a few hours since Sheila was sleeping and didn't notice her absence. But along with a sense of freedom, she felt even more guilt. Kendra wondered if she didn't love her sister because she was so happy to be away from her for a little while. She couldn't recall the last time she had a day when she wasn't

---

[130] Adam Palmer, "The Challenges Facing a Family Caregiver," *Senior Living & Nursing Homes in Indiana | ASC* (blog), March 30, 2021, https://www.asccare.com/the-challenges-facing-a-family-caregiver/.
[131] User USofCare, "Listening to Informal Caregivers: Outstanding Challenges and Needs," United States of Care, September 19, 2022, https://unitedstatesofcare.org/listening-to-informal-caregivers-outstanding-challenges-and-needs/.

sad, mad, frustrated, or ashamed, and those feelings were only compounded when she thought to herself how terrible she would feel once Sheila was gone.

Of all the complex emotions that accompany caregiving, one of the most burdensome is guilt. Guilt is common because caregivers often have unrealistic expectations of themselves, and they feel inadequate when they don't meet those expectations. Recognizing guilt when it shows up is essential so the caregiver can keep it from impacting the patient's quality of care. As a caregiver, it's important to determine how to realistically assess and reassess your abilities to create a healthy balance in your life.

Caregiver guilt is "a negative manifestation of the distress experienced when caring for a loved one," and it can include feeling depressed, burdened, or anxious. Some caregivers feel like they're not doing enough for the patient, may feel wrong about the changing roles in the relationship, and may feel inadequate for neglecting other aspects of life to provide care. Sometimes, the patient's high expectations or other people's inappropriate judgments make the caregiver feel guilty. Caregiving is as hard as it is beautiful and necessary, and its difficulties can bring mental exhaustion. It means juggling multiple tasks, roles, and responsibilities while neglecting other things you are responsible for. It can invite self-blame if the caregiver wrongly thinks they could have done something to improve the patient's condition. It can bring unresolved relationships to the surface and resentment for losing personal time they thought they would be spending in other ways. Finally, guilt can arise if and when the time comes to place the patient in a care facility if your capacity to look after your loved one runs out. Here are several ways caregivers can cope with these emotions:

1. **Identify when guilt occurs.** Permit yourself to admit your feelings and give yourself space and grace to feel that way. Don't judge yourself harshly. You're a human going through a challenging experience.

2. **Re-evaluate your expectations.** Ask yourself what is reasonable to request of yourself. You can do something, but you can't do everything.

3. **Don't stifle your feelings.** As a caregiver, anger, frustration, and confusion are all normal. There will be moments when you don't want to be a caregiver. Contact a therapist to help you work through your feelings if you need to.

4. **Connect with others.** Reach out to somebody. It can be a friend, family member, or a support group—someone you can talk to about challenging moments without hiding how you really feel.

5. **Make time for yourself.** You still have your own life. Live it as best you can and do that guilt-free.

6. **Go to group therapy.** Group therapy helps broaden your perspective and helps you realize you're not in this situation alone. Hearing firsthand what other people are going through can normalize your feelings. If you can't leave the house easily, online support groups are available.

7. **Be kind to yourself and accept that you're human.** Treat yourself with the same kindness and compassion you would treat a friend with if they were going through what you're going through. Be proactive in your self-care and be on the lookout for symptoms of caregiver burnout.

8. **Focus on quality time and find joy in the small moments.** When you compound your thoughts with what's already happening and what could happen, you compound your troubles. Today has enough trouble of its own, but it also has beauty if you're able to see it. Look for joy in the present moment.

9. **Remind yourself of all the positive things you've done.** When you're tired and overwhelmed, it can be hard to remember all the good you've done. Make a list or keep a journal of the good things you do and the good things that happen each day so you can look at them to remind yourself of the positive aspects of your relationship with your loved one.

10. **Don't internalize your loved one's negative behavior.** Dementia can change your loved one's brain chemistry to the point where their negative behavior can become focused on you in the form of name-calling or accusations. It's important to remember to let go of such behaviors. This version of them is not an accurate representation of how they really feel towards you.

11. **Be confident in your decisions.** Whatever choices you make, you're doing what you feel is best with the information available to you at the time. If things change, just remember that the choices you made before were made under different circumstances.

Guilt is a significant contributor to caregiver burnout, so the sooner you recognize the symptoms and seek help, the better. If these emotions are left to rot, they can lead to isolation, irritability, anger, depression, and other negative emotions that can cause emotional and even physical harm to the patient and yourself. Caregivers need to have someone to talk to. Mental health professionals are a great option, as they can help caregivers process their emotions, set realistic boundaries and expectations, and add balance to their lives. Therapists can also teach coping and problem-solving skills that will serve caregivers long-term. When choosing a therapist, look for one who's familiar with the needs of caregivers and who's empathetic to your plight. Check to see if your insurance will help cover the cost. [132]

We've all heard the saying, "You can't pour from an empty cup." If you don't take care of yourself, you'll have nothing to give. Too often, we confuse practicality for selfishness, but everyone else benefits when we take care of ourselves first. According to Caregiver.org, "If you are a caregiving spouse between the ages of 66 and 96 and are experiencing mental or emotional strain, you have a risk of dying that is 63 percent higher than people your age who are not caregivers." Self-care is a life-and-death situation. Let's explore ways that you can look after yourself while looking after your loved one.

---

[132] Choosing Therapy, "Caregiver Guilt: Causes, Getting Help, & How to Cope," February 16, 2024, https://www.choosingtherapy.com/caregiver-guilt/.

- **Take responsibility for your own care.** You can't do anything about the illness plaguing the patient you're caring for, but you can take responsibility for your own well-being and do what is necessary to ensure you stay in good health.

- **Identify personal barriers.** Many childhood beliefs influence us into our later years. These beliefs sometimes form barriers that prevent us from caring for ourselves. Instead of seeing self-care as self-centered, ask yourself what good you'll be to the patient if you become ill or die. Your mind tends to believe what you tell it, so instead of blaming yourself and sitting in frustration, remind yourself that you're doing your best with what you have. You're human, and you need to take time for yourself so you can show up as the best version of yourself.

- **Move forward.** Once you know your barriers to self-care, you can take steps to remove them.

Those steps can include:

1. **Reducing personal stress by recognizing warning signs** early on like irritability, sleep problems, and forgetfulness and acting on them immediately. Figure out what's causing your stress in the first place and make adjustments. Identify what you can and cannot change, and remember, the only person you can control is yourself. When you can, take action to reduce stress and do whatever works for you. This may include exercising regularly, practicing mindfulness and meditation, ensuring proper sleep, eating healthily, connecting with others, limiting screen time, engaging in relaxation techniques, pursuing hobbies, having pets, and seeking professional help.

2. **Setting goals for what you want to accomplish over the next 3-6 months.** You can take a break from caregiving through securing respite care, recruiting someone to help you with caregiving tasks, and engaging in activities that make you feel healthier. Break your goals

into small steps to give yourself some quick wins and make the goals more attainable.

3. **Seeking solutions to problems that feel overwhelming.** Identify the problem, list some possible solutions, select a solution, and try it. Once you've tested it, evaluate the results and if not ideal, try a different solution. Fine-tune the solution and make adjustments as necessary. Ask for input from others who might have helpful ideas, and if nothing seems to help, accept that the problem might not yet be solvable and choose to revisit it later.

   Raquel was adamant about cooking her mother's meals at home. She refused to let her mother eat any fast food, anything fried, anything microwavable, or anything sugary. Her intentions were good, but cooking three meals each day in addition to the other uncountable tasks on her plate was wearing her out. She considered asking family members to pitch in, but she didn't trust they would follow the guidelines she suggested. She thought about food prepping on Sundays, but again, time was a real factor. She brought up her dilemma at a support group meeting, and someone suggested subscribing to a meal prep service. She found one that was within her budget and provided nutrient-dense meals. To her surprise they were delicious, and her mother looked forward to them. Finding ways to make your life easier will pay massive dividends to your mental health.

4. **Communicating constructively** by using "I" statements instead of "you" statements (*I feel angry* instead of *You're making me angry*), respecting the way other people feel, expressing yourself clearly and precisely, and being a good listener can drastically reduce the friction in your relationship with your loved one.

5. **Asking for help and accepting it.** It is unrealistic to think you can handle all caregiver responsibilities independently. If you don't have a support system of friends or family willing to pitch in, seek help from other resources, like professionals. If you have a support system of

people willing to help, ask and be specific. Ask people to do what they enjoy (preparing meals, spending time with the patient playing games, etc.), and prepare a list of what needs to be done. Avoid asking the same person repeatedly and pick a good time to ask and make a plan of action with the helper. Be prepared for hesitance or refusal, and don't take it personally if that happens. Finally, be respectful and direct with your ask.

6. **Talking to the doctor.** You and the patient will spend a lot of time in the physician's office. Don't hesitate to ask any questions you have about the patient's condition, progression, or medications. You can also ask the physician about what you are feeling and experiencing as a caregiver. Make a list of questions that come up between visits so you don't forget what you want to ask. You can also ask the nurse, who is well-informed and ready to help. Take a friend with you for support and "memory back-up."

7. **Exercising** to promote better sleep, increased energy and alertness, and reduced tension and depression is one of the best things you can do for yourself. Exercise is available through an array of activities. You can ride a bike, lift weights, do yoga or Pilates, or even do chores or garden. Walking is a great way to get started and clear your mind, and you can do it outside or indoors in places like malls and grocery stores.

8. **Learning from your emotions provides invaluable lessons.** Emotions are powerful signposts that let us know when we need to slow down and pay attention. They're tools that help us understand what's happening externally and internally. Your emotions might tell you that it's time for a change in the caregiving situation, that you're grieving some sort of loss, that you're stressed out, or that it's time to get assertive about your needs.

Caregiver guilt can present at any time on the caregiver role trajectory. You might find yourself feeling guilty about not noticing your own symptoms and getting help sooner. You may feel inadequate in providing the care your loved one needs or in your ability to heal them with your efforts. You might feel guilty for not spending enough time with them in the past or while you've been working so hard to provide for their needs throughout the course of the illness. Remember, these feelings are normal, and it's important to remember what you can and cannot control. The only real control is self-control, and the best way to exhibit self-control through this experience is through self-care so you can be in the best condition possible to carry out your role as a caregiver. As a reminder, here are a list of ways you can do just that:

- Take time for yourself. Don't get into the habit of thinking you can't do anything for relief until "this is all over."

- Eat a balanced diet, drink plenty of water, and exercise.

- Get enough sleep, and schedule rest breaks throughout the day.

- Set limits for what you can do yourself, and make sure your schedule is realistic.

- Keep the lines of communication open with your support system and ask for help when or before you need it.

- Share your feelings with someone you trust. Caregiving is a heavy load you shouldn't try to shoulder alone.

- Give yourself credit. You're doing good work, and it makes a difference.[133]

- Set boundaries with the patient and your support system so no one expects you to be all things to all people all the time.[134]

---

[133] UCSF Health, "Self-Care for Caregivers," ucsfhealth.org, May 8, 2023, https://www.ucsfhealth.org/education/self-care-for-caregivers.
[134] Sarah Cornell LCSW, "Finding Balance: Tips for Managing Caregiving and Self-care," Mayo Clinic Health System, June 30, 2023, https://www.mayoclinichealthsystem.org/hometown-health/featured-topic/caregiving-self-care-during-beyond-the-covid-19-pandemic.

- Finally, if you feel overwhelmed and need someone to talk to, call or text 988 to reach the Suicide and Crisis Lifeline. Help is available 24/7.

Take Action

Review the lists in this chapter and highlight five things you can do to improve your mental, physical, and emotional well-being. You matter just as much as the patient!

In the next and final chapter, we'll explore what it looks like when the caregiver can no longer provide the care the patient needs. If it comes to this, you'll be equipped for the necessary next steps to ensure your loved one is in a place where they can receive the best care possible.

CHAPTER 11

When It's Beyond Your Control

I walked into the exam room to find Kendra and Sheila smiling. I hadn't seen Kendra smile in months. She looked fresh, her shoulders were relaxed, and she greeted me with brightness in her eyes.

"How are you?" I asked, excited to hear her response.

"Fantastic!" she answered.

Since our last visit, Kendra and Sheila had agreed that it was time for Sheila to move into a long-term care facility. She'd fallen several more times since the fall that caused the cut on her arm, and the alarm on the door was ringing more and more since her wandering had increased. In her frustration, Sheila was becoming more verbally aggressive towards Kendra, which was wearing on Kendra's self-esteem. She felt ill-equipped to do anything for her sister, even the things she'd been doing for months with no problem. She'd had thoughts of getting in her car and driving until she ran out of road, but she knew that wouldn't solve any issues. When Kendra expressed to me that she couldn't go any further caring for her sister as she had been, I walked her through the process of admitting it might be time to hand her sister's care over to someone else and search for the place that could do it best.

When do you know?

There is no definitive step in the progression of dementia when a caregiver should make the decision to place the patient in a long-term care facility. This point will come at a different time for everyone. There are guidelines, however, that can provide some clarity to the caregiver about whether the time has arrived.

Safety is priority one. Suppose you see that your loved one's behavior is no longer conducive to living alone or to your capacity to continue to care for them. In that case, it's time to consider placing them in a facility. The decision won't be easy, especially if other family members disagree. In this case, everyone involved in the decision should invite a doctor or senior care specialist into the decision-making process to provide the authority of a professional opinion.

A professional will look for signs that it's time for the patient to enter long-term care, like whether the patient often gets lost or agitated or has lost the ability to carry on a conversation. Other signs are that the patient looks disheveled or has lost weight. The doctor will try to get a feel for how the senior carries out daily activities. If they struggle to remember when to eat or drink, have difficulty dressing appropriately for the weather, can't bathe regularly or thoroughly, or have incontinence concerns, the doctor might suggest a mental status exam. If the patient leaves appliances on after cooking, has been to the emergency room more frequently, has bruises they can't explain, has been wandering, or needs help taking scheduled medications, it may be time for memory care. Keep in mind that this decision is not just for safety's sake; it's also a legal decision. Leaving a family member with dementia to care for themselves could become a legal issue, falling under the umbrella of elder abuse or neglect.

A mental status test only takes a few minutes and can be done in the doctor's office. It measures concentration, short-term memory, and spatial awareness. If the patient can communicate, the exam can provide a baseline for tracking dementia symptoms. The doctor will have the patient repeat words and then remember them later in the appointment, spell simple words backward, add and subtract simple equations, give objects their proper names, and understand visual and spatial cues, like where an object is located in the room. They will also ask questions to assess the patient's judgment in different scenarios. After the test, the patient may be referred to a neurologist or other specialist. These assessments clarify how much the patient's cognition has declined and the level of support they need. If keeping the patient safe, stimulated, and comfortable is not possible, it may be time to consider care outside the home.

Professional In-Home Care

One option to handle the burden of caregiving in advanced dementia is to recruit professional in-home care. They provide essential support to individuals with dementia, allowing them to maintain a sense of independence and comfort within their own homes. These services can be obtained through various channels, including private hires based on personal recommendations or word of mouth, online hiring platforms or social media, and professional agencies specializing in home care services. Private hires often allow for a more personal connection and potentially more flexibility in arranging care schedules, while agencies offer the advantage of pre-screened, trained caregivers who are matched to meet the specific needs of the individual with dementia. Agencies also provide a layer of oversight and accountability that can be reassuring for families.

There are several platforms and services that can help families find in-home care providers for individuals with dementia or other care needs. These platforms offer a range of options, from finding individual caregivers to connecting with professional agencies. Here are some notable ones:

1. **Care.com**: This is one of the largest and most well-known platforms for finding a variety of caregivers, including in-home care providers. Users can search for caregivers based on their specific needs, location, and other criteria. Care.com also offers background check options for added security.

THE PRACTICAL DEMENTIA CAREGIVER GUIDE

2. **Caring.com**: Specializing in senior care, Caring.com provides resources and listings for in-home care agencies, assisted living, and other elder care services. It also offers extensive guides and advice on choosing the right care options.

3. **HomeCare.com**: This platform focuses on connecting families with professional in-home caregivers. HomeCare.com pre-screens all caregivers and offers matching services based on the specific needs and preferences of the individual requiring care.

4. **AgingCare.com**: AgingCare.com offers a platform where families can find and hire caregivers, as well as access resources and support from a community of caregivers who share advice and experiences related to elder care.

5. **Honorcare.com**: As a tech-driven home care company, Honor partners with local agencies to provide a network of caregivers. They use technology to match care professionals with families based on specific care needs, preferences, and schedules.

6. **VisitingAngels.com**: One of the leading national home care franchises, Visiting Angels offers personalized in-home care services, including dementia care. They provide comprehensive caregiver screening and matching services.

7. **Sittercity.com**: Primarily known for babysitting, Sittercity also offers senior care services. The platform allows families to post jobs and interview candidates to find a caregiver who fits their needs.

When using these platforms, it's important for families to conduct their due diligence, such as checking references, conducting interviews, and ensuring that the caregiver or agency is a good fit for their specific situation. Additionally, considering the platform's reputation, the security measures they take in vetting caregivers, and the support they offer in case of issues can help make the process smoother and safer.

Paying for in-home care requires careful consideration of available resources and options. Medicaid can be a source of funding for those who meet the eligibility criteria, typically covering in-home care services for individuals with low income and assets. For those not eligible for Medicaid, paying out of pocket is an option, though it can be costly over time. Alternatively, some individuals may have secondary insurance to Medicare, such as Medigap or other private insurance policies, which can cover some if not all the cost of in-home care. However, it's important to note that these insurance plans often require that the in-home care services be obtained through Medicare licensed agencies to ensure the quality and legitimacy of the care provided.

Navigating the landscape of in-home care requires a balance of personal preferences, financial considerations, and the specific needs of the individual with dementia. Whether opting for a private caregiver or securing services through an agency, the goal is to ensure that the care provided enhances the quality of life for the person with dementia, offering support, companionship, and specialized care that addresses their unique challenges. You should explore all available options, including state and local resources, to make informed decisions that align with your financial situation and care requirements.

Questions to Ask

If professional in home care is not an option for you and you are considering moving your loved one to a care facility, here are some questions to ask yourself when considering such a big decision:

1. **Have friends or family members commented on changes in behavior?** As the caregiver who sees the patient all day, every day, it can be hard to notice changes that happen steadily over a span of time. However, people who see the patient sparingly can notice drastic changes more easily. For example, while Kendra noticed big things, like Sheila's loss of balance, she didn't notice how much weight Sheila had lost until Tyler pointed it out during one of his visits.

2. **Is the patient showing signs of agitation or aggression?** Changes in the patient's brain that make it difficult for them to express themselves can make them feel unsafe, resulting in agitated, aggressive, or violent behaviors. These behaviors can be dangerous, especially when the caregiver is also a senior. Sheila hadn't become physically violent towards Kendra, but her words had certainly become more hurtful. She couldn't carry on entire conversations like before, so she became sharp-tongued and negative when she was uncomfortable and needed to express that.

3. **Is your aging relative withdrawn or nervous?** Patients may decline social invitations and avoid their favorite activities.

4. **Are their hygiene needs met?** As dementia progresses, you may notice that someone who took great care of their appearance in the past no longer does. Also, incontinence might mean the patient is wearing soiled clothes, and the smell in their environment might quickly become unpleasant.

5. **Does your loved one wander?** This is a common sign that it's time for a memory care facility. Confusion or disorientation can cause a patient to wander far from home without realizing it, putting them in very dangerous situations. While locks and alarms can help minimize risks at home, care facilities have unique layouts that keep patients secure.

6. **Are their living conditions safe?** A patient may hoard household items, neglect cleaning, eat spoiled food, or forget to pick up pet waste. They might trip and fall often, misuse dangerous appliances or chemicals, or find themselves in other risky situations. As circumstances change, where the patient lives may need to change, too.

7. **Are their medications properly managed?** Forgetting to take medications or taking too much of a medication can lead to serious side effects. While schedules, alerts, and pill organizers might help

initially, patients usually need more intervention as their health declines.

8. **Is your loved one well-nourished?** Eating becomes a challenge as dementia progresses. Seniors with dementia may require special meal plans to help with other health conditions; they may overeat or forget to eat. This change may require special care to help avoid significant weight changes.

9. **Have you started to feel caregiver burnout?** Growing exhausted under the weight of caring for a loved one is perfectly human and normal. If these feelings go unaddressed, they can lead to more harm than the good you will be able to provide if you keep trucking along without intervention.

10. **Are you feeling resentful?** If you can't think of anything positive about the patient or the situation, or if you are overwhelmed with guilt, you might be burned out. Consider whether it's time to turn the brunt of caring for your loved one over to professionals.

11. **Is caregiving affecting your health?** Caregiver burnout can have severe physical and emotional consequences. If your health declines, you may end up putting yourself and the patient at risk.

12. **Are you and your family safe?** Aggression from a patient can put others in physical, sexual, or emotional danger. It may seem strange that someone you love so much and who loves you so much could put you in danger, but behavioral changes are due to changes in the brain that the patient can't control. If these behaviors turn violent, it's time to seek help.[135]

In its late stages, dementia might require around-the-clock care. Consider whether you can provide that in light of your other responsibilities, like work, family relationships, health, and ability to carry out the patient's medical and

---

[135] Chacour Koop, "Signs It's Time for Memory Care: 13 Questions to Ask," December 19, 2023, https://www.aplaceformom.com/caregiver-resources/articles/is-it-time-for-memory-care.

personal needs. Think about whether your home provides the necessary technological safety elements and therapies that a care facility does..[136] If not, and if you answered yes to any of the questions in the list above, understand that these factors are out of your control. At that point, it is smart, safe, and loving to hand over caring for your loved one to professionals equipped to handle these situations in an environment designed to provide the help your loved one needs. You may choose to get an in-home care professional or move your loved one to a facility depending on your preference, finances, and availability of resources.

Making the Memory Care Decision

It's best when the decision to move to a care facility is a shared decision. Caregivers should make an effort to involve the patient in the transition as much as possible instead of forcing them into a facility. The transition requires proactivity on your part in seeking support from others and helping to make the change as comfortable as possible for the patient. When the time comes to consider long-term care, follow these steps:

Step 1: Get support from family members.

Before speaking with the patient about moving to a care facility, reach out to any family members who may be involved in the decision. This way, you can all present a united front. If the people involved in the decision are divided, use the following strategies to make things easier.

- **Practice active listening.**

    When others express their feelings about the move, listen to hear what they're saying. Validate their opinions by using statements like, "I understand this is frustrating." Reword their statements so they know you're paying attention. You can recount their thoughts back to them by saying, "It sounds like you feel/think …" Doing this also helps

---

[136] "7 Signs It's Time for Memory Care," © 2007-2024 AgingCare All Rights Reserved., n.d., https://www.agingcare.com/articles/when-is-it-time-to-place-a-loved-one-with-dementia-188309.htm.

avoid misunderstandings. Use "I" statements instead of "you" statements like, "I feel like Mom/Dad isn't safe at home," and ask questions to show curiosity about their viewpoint like, "What concerns you most about Mom/Dad moving to long-term care?"

- **Seek a credible outside opinion.**

  When family members struggle to agree, a third party can provide insight that can lead to a consensus. This person might be someone who has experience in senior living, the patient's primary care physician, a geriatric care manager, or a neurologist. A medical professional can also provide an assessment to help family members solidify the decision to move the patient.

- **Detail the primary caregiver's experience.**

  Tensions often arise between the adult caregiver who's providing the brunt of the care and other adult siblings. As the primary caregiver, keep a journal and share updates about the patient's condition via email. This provides a higher level of awareness to family members about the patient's condition and serves as a paper trail.

Step 2: Tour memory care facilities on your own.

By exploring care facilities on your own, you can research the amenities and activities they offer that you think your loved one will appreciate. By touring facilities early in the process, the family can move the patient more quickly in case of a sudden decline in their health. We will talk about how to choose the right home for your loved one later in this chapter.

Step 3: Consider who to include in the conversation.

As you determine who should have a say in placing your loved one in a care facility, consider your family's dynamics. If the patient has a close relationship with multiple adult children, a collaborative family meeting may be appropriate so your loved one can hear different perspectives from everyone they trust.

Patients who are sensitive about their condition might prefer a one-on-one conversation with the primary family caregiver. If they are hostile, they might need to speak with a physician or healthcare provider because of their credibility. Suppose the patient requires care quickly due to an emergency. In that case, a one-on-one conversation may be the most efficient way to make a decision, as there may not be time to gather the entire family.

Step 4: Choose the right time and place.

Once you know who will participate in the conversation, you can make it more successful by having the conversation in the morning when your minds are sharp, choosing a comfortable and secure location, and using supportive body language and visual cues to get your point across.

Step 5: Establish a core line or script.

Before the family starts the conversation with the patient, they should agree on the core messaging of the conversation. Each member should avoid contributing information opposite to what someone else verbalizes, as such inconsistency can confuse and aggravate someone with memory loss. Keep the focus of the conversation on the care facility's social aspects, the patient's safety, and quality of life. Here are some guidelines to help you steer the conversation:

- **Focus on the benefits of memory care.**

    Telling patients about safety and staff friendliness can help them accept the situation. Once you let them know they'll be in a place where trained professionals will treat them right and offer the best care possible, the patient often feels more at ease. Even if they make a statement like, "You're not shipping me off to some nursing home," let them know things have changed significantly over the years. Facilities of today offer housekeeping, nutritious food, opportunities for them to socialize with other residents, and supportive, trained staff.

- **Talk about the plan for now, not forever.**

    Avoid panic by focusing on today instead of the rest of the patient's life. When patients think they're moving to a care facility forever, they are more likely to resist the move. However, when you frame the move as a temporary measure, your loved one's focus tends to be more on being in the facility today versus staying in the facility forever.

- **Don't make yourself the bad guy.**

    Shift responsibility for the decision to healthcare professionals instead of taking all of it upon yourself. If the patient doesn't want to go, let them know the doctor recommends this.

What to do when the patient says "no."

If you've done everything right, and the patient is still hesitant or hostile, don't worry; this is a common reaction. Doctors say you should expect pushback as the patient's initial response.

If you find yourself in the position of dealing with pushback:

1. **Try to understand the emotion beneath the reaction.** No one wants to give up their independence and leave their home. Empathizing with the patient about the unknown can reassure them.

2. **Put yourself in the patient's shoes.** As you know, once dementia hits a particular stage, the patient's thought processes will change. Consider how they would have reacted to the news before their health took a turn for the worse. Think about what you would want if you were the patient and someone had to make the same decision for your benefit.

In emergencies, families can lean on tools like power of attorney (POA) or guardianship that allow caregivers to make decisions on the patient's behalf when their memory or judgment is impaired.

Definitions:

- **Power of Attorney (POA):**

  A Power of Attorney is a legal document that grants one person, known as the agent or attorney-in-fact, the authority to make decisions and act on behalf of another person, known as the principal. The scope of authority granted by the POA can be broad or limited and typically includes managing financial affairs, making health care decisions, or handling specific tasks. The authority of the POA generally ceases if the principal becomes incapacitated, unless it is a durable power of attorney.

- **Durable Power of Attorney:**

  A Durable Power of Attorney is a specific type of Power of Attorney that remains in effect even if the principal becomes incapacitated or unable to make decisions for themselves. The "durable" aspect refers to the lasting power of the document under such circumstances. This type of POA is particularly important for long-term planning, as it ensures that the agent can continue to act on the principal's behalf if they are no longer mentally competent to handle their affairs.

- **Guardian:**

  While POA is appointed by an individual, guardianship is granted by the court when the patient can no longer make decisions about their own care. The guardian makes healthcare and financial decisions and ensures that the patient's day-to-day needs are met. Guardianship is typically established through a legal process where the court determines the incapacity of the individual and selects a suitable guardian. The guardian's decisions are subject to oversight by the court to ensure the best interests of the ward are being served. [137]

---

[137] Hca Dev, "How to Apply for Guardianship of a Parent With Dementia," Stowell Associates, March 9, 2022, https://stowellassociates.com/how-to-get-guardianship-of-parent-with-dementia/.

Find Support and Let Go of Guilt

Deciding when to place a loved one in a long-term care facility can be one of the most emotional experiences of the dementia care journey. As you take care of your loved one, check in with yourself. This is a great time to connect with in-person or online support groups, talk to a therapist or counselor, and remind yourself that placing your family member in a facility that can meet all their needs is an act of love._[138]

Things to Consider when Choosing a Home for Your Loved One

Choosing a long-term care facility for the patient in your care is an important decision that can seem overwhelming. That's why it's important to know what you're looking for in an ideal facility and to ask the right questions.

- **Choose which type of care facility is most appropriate**

    Residential care includes retirement housing, assisted living, nursing homes, memory care units, and continuing care retirement communities. Each type of facility is set up to cater to different needs, so consult your physician about which option would best fit your loved one.

- **Family Involvement**

    Ask about the facility's guidelines concerning family involvement. Do they encourage families of patients to participate in care planning? How do they alert families of changes in the patient's condition and needs? Does the staff encourage communication? If the facility does not encourage family involvement and an open line of communication,

---

[138] Kara Lewis, "How to Talk to Your Parent About Moving to Memory Care," January 31, 2024, https://www.aplaceformom.com/caregiver-resources/articles/how-to-talk-about-moving-to-memory-care.

you will likely feel unsure, stressed, and possibly even skeptical of how your loved one is being treated.

- **Staffing**

    One advantage of a care facility is that medical professionals are there to handle patients' medical needs, so ask questions about the extent of healthcare professional involvement on the premises. Does the facility provide medical care? How often are doctors and nurses present? Is a registered nurse at the facility at all times? If not, what is the facility's tie to a medical establishment? Does the facility offer hospice care? Is personal care provided, and if so, is it tailored to each patient's specific needs? Are staff specifically trained in dementia care? Are they equipped to handle challenging behaviors? What is the ratio of residents to staff? When you hand over care to someone else, you want to be assured that they are equipped for the job and that the right professionals will be on-site in case anything concerning happens. If the facility cannot guarantee this level of professional care, consider other options if you can.

- **Programs and Services**

    The patient's mental health and socialization are an essential part of their care plan, so learn all you can about the programs and services the facility offers. Are the appropriate services and programming available to patients based on their specific health and behavioral care needs, like small groups or quiet rooms? Are there planned activities, and can you look at a schedule to see what they consist of? Is transportation available for medical appointments and shopping? Are any therapies like physical, speech, occupational, or recreational offered to residents? Are religious services and celebrations offered? It's important for patients to feel like life continues after they move into a new residence. If there are limited to no programs like this available at a facility, it becomes easier for patients to fall into depression and feelings of isolation.

- **Residents**

    Caring for your loved one's dignity is paramount when choosing a long-term care facility. Ask questions about how the staff handles residents. When it comes to personal care like bathing, grooming, and toileting, do they perform it with respect and dignity? Is there an extra financial charge per service? Is the staff willing to maintain the schedule you'd already established in the care environment at home? Are residents comfortable and relaxed? Do they participate in the activities the facility offers? How often do residents experience falls in the facility? Are residents with psychiatric illness as their primary diagnosis sharing the same unit as those with dementia? Nothing is more important than your loved one's safety and well-being, so do not be shy about questions like this. If for any reason you feel uncomfortable or that your needs won't be met, ask more questions for clarity, or keep scouting facilities until one feels more like home.

- **Environment**

    One reason people feel cautious about care facilities is because of the idea that these facilities feel cold and unpleasant. Times have changed, and one of the first things you'll notice is how cozy these places can be. Some things to notice as you explore: Is the facility free of odors? Are the rooms clean and spacious? Do indoor spaces allow for freedom of movement and promote independence, and are all spaces safe, secure, and monitored? Is there a designated visiting area for visitors? Can residents bring familiar items from home, like photos and bedding? Some places even allow pets! The warmer the environment, the better both you and the patient will feel about the move. Also, ask about isolation and visitation protocols for communicable infections like influenza, COVID-19, gastrointestinal diseases, etc.

- **Meals**

    Food is vital to a patient's physical, mental, and emotional health. Their nutrition is a vital component of their care plan, and food that tastes good directly affects emotions and feelings of care and belonging. Find out the rules and guidelines concerning food at the facilities you tour. Are there regularly scheduled meals and snack times, and are those times flexible to align with the patient's schedule? Can you see and even sample from a menu of the food? Are meals tailored to the patient's needs? Are there environmental distractions at mealtimes? Are family and friends allowed to join the patient for meals?[139] The correct answers to these questions will provide comfort for the patient and, as a result, comfort for you about your loved one's care.

- **Ratings**

    In the United States, you can check the Medicare providers comparison tool to see how any nursing care facilities you're exploring rank on a scale of one to five. Facilities rated a one have below average ratings, while those rated a five have the highest. Ratings for independent Memory Care facilities can be found on various sites, the best of which are local and regional listings.

Keep in mind that these ratings may not guarantee that the facility has everything you're looking for, so don't let the rating tell the whole story.[140] As you explore different facilities, establish guidelines for important factors in a care facility versus deal-breakers. There are some elements you may be willing to compromise on and others that absolutely must be present. You might accept a good or great facility if you can't find one that's perfect, so determine your non-negotiables as you explore all the options.

---

[139] Alzheimer's Association, "Choosing a Residential Care Community," 2023, https://www.alz.org/media/documents/alzheimers-dementia-choosing-residential-care-ts.pdf.
[140] "Five-Star Quality Rating System | CMS," n.d., https://www.cms.gov/medicare/health-safety-standards/certification-compliance/five-star-quality-rating-system.

Scan the QR code below to access the Medicare providers comparison tool.

https://www.medicare.gov/care-compare/

- **Costs**

    Assess the complete financial outlay. Know what your loved one's insurance will cover, if anything, and know all the costs. For example, most assisted living and memory care facilities require a down payment that is refundable if you change your mind and don't place your loved one in the facility. Once you do place your loved one, however, they usually also require a "community fee" that is not refundable once the patient moves in. High costs could be a real challenge for many families. If affordability of the facility is an issue for you, I suggest that you 1. seek advice on local programming and financial assistance from the state's Department of Aging and 2. Once you find the funds, seek full time in-home care, which is way more affordable than a facility. Bear in mind that in many cases, if your patient is admitted directly from hospital to nursing care, the Medicare and secondary insurance kick in and make it way more affordable.

- **Preparing for the Move**

    Many facilities will visit your loved one at home or in the hospital, or they might invite them to see the home before they move in. If this is allowed, speak with a staff member to inform them about the patient. You can also compile a record of the patient's life to help make the transition easier. Explore the possibility of arranging a short respite stay. If the patient likes the facility, they may have no issue moving in. On the day of the move, try to keep the environment as stress and conflict-free as possible and make the patient's room comfortable and reminiscent of home.

- **Remember Yourself**

    Moving your loved one into a facility can be emotionally challenging. You might feel like you've lost them or let them down. You might feel lonely or isolated. You might even feel guilty if you feel relief from your caregiving role. All of these feelings are normal. Try to ease back into the life you had before caregiving became your top priority, and keep in mind that because you're no longer the primary caregiver, your time with the patient can be more enjoyable and less stressful.[141]

Before Kendra made the ultimate decision to transfer Sheila to a long-term care facility, she felt guilty even thinking about it. She decided to compile a list of the pros and cons of continuing care at home. That's when the reality of the situation moved from abstract thoughts and emotions to a black-and-white synopsis that she could look at on paper and know was real. During a previous visit, I asked her, "If this were someone else, and you were looking at this same piece of paper with these same facts, what would you recommend to this caregiver?"

"I'd tell them to get help yesterday!" she answered.

"You deserve that same help, Kendra," I told her.

And so do you.

If you find yourself struggling with feelings of guilt, open up to someone you trust. If you have someone you can reach out to who's been in the same situation, contact them to talk things through. Via honest dialogue, you might

---

[141] "Considering a Care Home for a Person With Dementia - Dementia UK," Dementia UK, n.d., https://www.dementiauk.org/information-and-support/specialist-diagnosis-and-support/considering-a-care-home-for-a-person-with-dementia/.

find comfort in knowing you can let go. If you find yourself going back on a promise that putting your loved one elsewhere for their care was something you'd never do, remember, circumstances change. When they do, decisions may have to change along with them.

Even when placing a loved one in a care home is the best rational decision, it can be hard to let go of your responsibilities. You may feel like you didn't do enough or abandoned your loved one. Managing the guilt of the decision is an ongoing process, so start with figuring out what triggers these feelings in you and detaching your emotions from the rationality of the decision. Remember that what is best might not always feel best, and your best might not be enough anymore. Once you've accepted that you can no longer meet their needs and that workers in the care facility are professionals, you can more easily settle into your new role: a dementia patient's loved one who now has less pressure and responsibility, which means more capacity for love and empathy. When you see the facility is doing a great job meeting your loved one's needs, you'll feel much more confident in your decision. Still, if by chance you don't feel that way, let's explore some ways to cope with the guilt of placing your loved one in a care home.

- **Realize that they're in good hands.** The purpose of a care home is to provide care for those who need it. The one you choose will be run by vetted professionals trained to look after the patients' needs around the clock.

- **Think of the benefits of living in a care facility.** Patients can socialize, participate in activities, eat good food, and have access to medical care when they need it. They may even be able to improve their independence.

- **Take care of yourself.** Caregiving can consume you and have adverse effects on your well-being. Allow yourself the space and freedom to resume your lifestyle and relationships, which is most likely what your loved one would want you to do. Remember, your needs are just as important as anybody else's.

- **Talk to someone.** Don't keep your feelings to yourself. Guilt is common, which means you're not alone. Find support in others who've been through it, and if you need to, seek the help of a mental health professional.[142]

Unfortunately, not all patients will go into long-term care willingly. Dementia patients might be particularly resistant to change, and transitioning their living environment might be very stressful. If this is the case, keeping your emotions, especially guilt, in check is especially important. Just because they don't like the change doesn't mean it's not the best decision. It's best to begin discussions about the possibility of moving early so it's not jolting when the time comes. Do your due diligence so you can present your loved one with the facts about the facilities you're considering. What's most important is that they are in a place where they can best have their needs met.[143]

Take Action

I hope that when the time comes to consider moving your loved one to a care facility outside of the home, you will feel empowered to make the best decision about how their care will progress. Knowing the signs to look for in the patient, the support you'll need from your family, and the necessary features for a suitable new living space helps to bring clarity where emotions could otherwise take over. Go back through this chapter and highlight the signs your loved one might be displaying or the signs in yourself that speak to caregiver burnout that might suggest it's time for a change.

By now, I hope your understanding of the realities of dementia is less mysterious. This illness brings many dynamic changes to the patient, the

---

[142] Viktor Berg, "How to Cope with the Guilt of Putting Someone in a Care Home," Carehome.co.uk, August 1, 2023, https://www.carehome.co.uk/advice/how-to-cope-with-the-guilt-of-putting-a-loved-one-in-a-care-home.

[143] ConnorFewings, "Dealing With the Guilt of Putting Your Parent in a Nursing Home," First Class Nursing & Care Homes in North Devon and Somerset, April 4, 2018, https://eastleighcarehomes.co.uk/blog/how-to-deal-with-the-guilt-of-putting-your-parent-in-a-nursing-home/#:~:text=how%20you%20feel.-,Dealing%20with%20the%20guilt%20of%20putting%20a%20parent%20in%20a,to%20a%20mental%20health%20professional.

patient's family, and everyone in the patient's support system. Fortunately, knowledge is one of the best forms of support. Now that you know what dementia does to the brain, how it progresses, how to adjust to your role as a caregiver, strategies to make it through challenging days, how to care for yourself as you care for your loved one, and what is and is not in your control, you can use this knowledge to make calculated decisions that will provide the best possible outcomes for everyone who will be touched by your loved one's dementia diagnosis. As you prepare for the dementia caregiving journey, use this guide as a reference as often as you need.

Above all, remember to care for yourself. This journey is not easy, and it can last for years. Nonetheless, by using the information in this book and taking things one day at a time, you can serve your role as a caregiver for the long term, and you can do so without discouragement and burnout. When you start to feel like it's all too much, do not hesitate to reach out to the wealth of supportive people and organizations created solely to walk this path alongside you. Caregiving is a noble act. Neglecting your own self-care is not.

Thank you for taking on the responsibility of caring for your loved one as they travel down this scary road. You are a champion. You will be the one championing your loved one's needs and wants. You'll be an advocate and a shoulder to lean on, often on the same day. You'll discover parts of yourself you may not have known existed, and you'll always be a winner in your loved one's story. While their mind might not always remember you, their heart will.

Conclusion

Do you remember the story, "Stone Soup"?
A man was traveling and stopped into a village for the night. He knocked on the door of a house, and a woman answered. He explained to her that he was traveling and needed a place to stay. She said he could stay, but she didn't have much food to eat. In fact, no one did because the harvest had been weak that year.

"That's okay," he responded. "I like to eat stone soup."

"You can't make soup out of stone," she scoffed.

"Yes, I can, if you'll just give me a pot and some water."

The lady gave him a pot and water, which he put on the stove and dropped his stone inside. He tasted the soup.

"How is it?" she asked.

"It's fine, but it would be better with some salt," he responded.

"I have some salt!" she answered.

The traveler added the salt to the soup. Just then, a neighbor knocked on the door.

"What are you doing?" he asked.

"We're making stone soup," said the traveler.

"Stone soup? I've never had it," said the neighbor, confused.

"Well, you should try it. It's decent, but it would be much better with a few carrots."

"I've got a carrot!"

The neighbor ran home, returned, and added carrots to the soup.

A woman walking down the street overheard the conversation and dropped in.

"Stone soup, you say? What is this?" she asked.

"It's a delicious soup!" said the neighbor.

"Oh yes, but it would be even more delicious with a bit of cabbage and an onion," added the traveler.

The lady reached into her bag and said, "I've got a bit of cabbage right here, and an onion, too!" and handed them over to be added to the pot.

The man down the street smelled the soup from his front porch and made his way to the house.

"What are you making here?" he asked.

"Stone soup," said the lady who'd given the cabbage and onion.

"It's delightful, but it would be outstanding with some chicken," he suggested.

"I'll be right back!" said the man from down the street. He ran home and grabbed a slaughtered chicken. He came back and dropped his chicken into the pot.

The homeowner's mother stopped by for her evening visit. She asked what they were making.

"Stone soup!" said everyone in unison.

"It's amazing, but you know what would make it gourmet? Beans," she said.

The mother went home and came right back with a bag of beans to add to the pot.

The group talked and laughed until the meal was done, and the traveler served everyone from the pot of delicious soup.

"Do tell us, where did you get that magical stone?" asked one of the neighbors, slurping the soup into his mouth.

"It's not the stone that's magic; your willingness to give made the soup special."

The following day, the traveler packed his things and left. The host thanked him for making the best meal anyone on the street had had in months.

He grabbed his bag, tipped his hat, and replied, "When everyone gives a bit of what they have, everyone ends up with more than they thought they had." And he went ahead on his journey.

It may seem like dementia is solely a taker. It takes memories, personalities, and time. But it also provides an opportunity for everyone who loves the patient to contribute in whatever way they can, which helps to bring the family together and makes the situation more bearable for everyone. Dementia is indeed confusing, challenging, and downright brutal at times, and it's also true that there's no one-size-fits-all solution for navigating the ups and downs of caregiving. Just know that you are not alone, and resources like the ones in this book and a solid support system can give you the strength to push through.

Six years from the first time I met Sheila and Kendra, I ran into Kendra at the grocery store. She was in a bit of a hurry. It was her birthday, and she was picking up a few things she needed for her party. As we were talking, Tyler rounded the corner and joined the conversation.

"It's good to see you both! How have you been?" I asked.

"I'm doing really well," smiled Kendra. "I used to feel bad saying that, but not anymore. I'm exercising again, I'm in touch with my friends, and I've decided to start doing anything that comes to mind that makes me feel alive," she said.

"It's her birthday. We're having a big party!" added Tyler.

"Happy birthday!" I said.

"Thank you. I never really got a chance to thank you for everything, as a matter of fact. You helped me so much. I didn't know where to start when we found out Sheila had dementia, but with the information you gave me, I was able to take care of my sister the way I knew she wanted and needed to be taken care of. When I couldn't do it myself anymore, I knew what to do, instead. When her fight was over, once I got past the initial grief, I was able to look back and see that we'd handled her with all the love and dignity she deserved," said Kendra.

"Not only that, but Aunt Kendra was a rockstar. I was paying attention to her every step of the way, and now, if I'm ever in that position, I'll know what to do," added Tyler.

I left that conversation knowing that with the right information, we can do anything.

Now that you can spot the symptoms of dementia, you understand its causes, and you know the value of early intervention, you'll feel less intimidated to talk to your loved one about it. You'll have a greater understanding of your loved one's behavioral changes, and you'll be more empathetic to what they're going through. You'll more readily move towards a place of acceptance of the situation instead of resistance, which will prepare you to lead difficult conversations about your loved one's care. You now know how to make adjustments to your loved one's home and lifestyle to keep them as safe as possible, and you have a toolbox of strategies to help you communicate with them more effectively all the way through the late stages of their condition. When their condition changes with the progression of the disease, you'll know how to manage their challenging behaviors. You know the importance of

THE PRACTICAL DEMENTIA CAREGIVER GUIDE

spending quality time with your loved one and how doing so contributes to their joy and yours, and by now, your role and responsibilities as their caregiver are clear. You've discovered strategies to avoid burnout and find balance, and you know how to assess your capabilities to continue your loved one's care as things become more challenging in dementia's late stages. Fear usually comes from what we do not know. Now that you know these things, hopefully, you're feeling more empowered and less helpless.

I hope the information and stories in this guide will help you overcome the struggles of caring for a loved one with dementia. May the strength you find here enable you to become a source of comfort and stability for your loved one.

I'm rooting for you.

Passing the Torch of Care

Now that you've armed yourself with the knowledge to provide unparalleled care for your loved one with dementia without feeling overwhelmed or lost, it's time to share your journey and insights. Your honest review of this book on Amazon can guide other caregivers to this valuable resource, empowering them to offer the same level of compassionate care to their loved ones.

By sharing your thoughts, you're not just reviewing a book; you're lighting the way for others navigating the challenging path of dementia caregiving. Your input can make a real difference in the lives of countless families, showing them they're not alone in their journey.

Thank you for joining me in this mission. Together, by sharing our knowledge, we ensure that effective and heartfelt care for those with dementia continues to thrive. You are a crucial part of this continuing legacy.

Scan the QR code below to leave your review on Amazon.

https://www.amazon.com/review/review-your-purchases/?asin=B0D2JMJSSV

A Special GIFT for You!

As a token of my gratitude for purchasing this book, I am delighted to offer you a special gift.

"Nourishing the Mind: *A Caregiver's Guide to Diet and Nutrition for Dementia"* is an essential guide that offers expert nutritional advice to improve brain health. It focuses on optimal hydration and easy-to-swallow meals and provides numerous recipes tailored to meet the unique needs of dementia patients, boosting their cognitive function.

Scan the QR code below to Download your FREE copy now!

https://savvyscrolls.net/dementia

References

Abraldes, Peter R. "Patience When Caring for Someone Living With Dementia - NursePartners, Inc." *NursePartners, Inc* (blog), February 20, 2018. https://www.nursepartners.org/patience-caring-for-someone-living-with-dementia/.

Admin. "The Important of Routine and Familiarity to Persons With Dementia." Alzheimers Project, June 7, 2020. https://alzheimersproject.org/the-importance-of-routine-and-familiarity-to-persons-with-dementia/.

Agency for Integrated Care. "Help Loved One Accept Dementia Diagnosis - Agency for Integrated Care," August 12, 2023. https://www.aic.sg/caregiving/help-loved-one-accept-dementia-diagnosis/.

Age Space. "What Is the Life Expectancy for Someone With Dementia?," January 19, 2024. https://www.agespace.org/dementia/life-expectancy#:~:text=Type%20of%20Dementia,-The%20type%20of&text=%2D%208%20to%2012%20years.

Alzheimer's Association. "Choosing a Residential Care Community," 2023. https://www.alz.org/media/documents/alzheimers-dementia-choosing-residential-care-ts.pdf.

Alzheimer's Disease and Dementia. "Accepting the Diagnosis," n.d. https://www.alz.org/help-support/caregiving/stages-behaviors/accepting_the_diagnosis.

Alzheimer's Disease and Dementia. "Alzheimer's Disease Facts and Figures," n.d. https://www.alz.org/alzheimers-dementia/facts-figures#:~:text=About%201%20in%209%20people,other%20dementias%20as%20older%20Whites.

Alzheimer's Disease and Dementia. "Bathing," n.d. https://www.alz.org/help-support/caregiving/daily-care/bathing.

Alzheimer's Disease and Dementia. "Chronic Traumatic Encephalopathy (CTE)," n.d. https://www.alz.org/alzheimers-dementia/what-is-dementia/related_conditions/chronic-traumatic-encephalopathy.

Alzheimer's Disease and Dementia. "Daily Care Plan," n.d. https://www.alz.org/help-support/caregiving/daily-care/daily-care-plan.

Alzheimer's Disease and Dementia. "Financial Planning," n.d. https://www.alz.org/help-support/i-have-alz/plan-for-your-future/financial_planning.

Alzheimer's Research UK. "What Is Frontotemporal Dementia? | Alzheimer's Research UK," January 24, 2024. https://www.alzheimersresearchuk.org/dementia-information/types-of-dementia/frontotemporal-dementia/#:~:text=Frontotemporal%20dementia%2C%20also%20known%20as,younger%20or%20older%20than%20this.

Alzheimer's Society. "Aggressive Behaviour and Dementia," December 13, 2021. https://www.alzheimers.org.uk/about-dementia/symptoms-and-diagnosis/symptoms/aggressive-behaviour-and-dementia.

Alzheimer's Society. "Alcohol-related 'Dementia,'" n.d. https://www.alzheimers.org.uk/about-dementia/types-dementia/alcohol-related-dementia.

Alzheimer's Society. "Can Genes Cause Dementia?," October 8, 2021. https://www.alzheimers.org.uk/about-dementia/risk-factors-and-prevention/can-genes-cause-dementia.

Alzheimer's Society. "Communicating and Dementia," n.d. https://www.alzheimers.org.uk/about-dementia/symptoms-and-diagnosis/symptoms/communicating-and-dementia.

Alzheimer's Society. "Delusions, Paranoia and Dementia," February 26, 2021. https://www.alzheimers.org.uk/about-dementia/symptoms-and-diagnosis/delusions.

Alzheimer's Society. "Dementia and Language," n.d. https://www.alzheimers.org.uk/about-dementia/symptoms-and-diagnosis/symptoms/dementia-and-language#content-start.

Alzheimer's Society. "Dementia Symptoms and Areas of the Brain," n.d. https://www.alzheimers.org.uk/about-dementia/symptoms-and-diagnosis/how-dementia-progresses/symptoms-brain#content-start.

Alzheimer's Society. "Explanation of the Functions of the Brain," March 18, 2021. https://www.alzheimers.org.uk/about-dementia/symptoms-and-diagnosis/how-dementia-progresses/function-brain#content-start.

Alzheimer's Society. "Hallucinations and Dementia," February 26, 2021. https://www.alzheimers.org.uk/about-dementia/symptoms-and-diagnosis/hallucinations.

Alzheimer's Society. "How Does Dementia Affect Sex and Intimacy?," n.d. https://www.alzheimers.org.uk/get-support/daily-living/sex-intimacy-dementia#content-start.

Alzheimer's Society. "How to Communicate With a Person With Dementia," December 20, 2021. https://www.alzheimers.org.uk/about-dementia/symptoms-and-diagnosis/symptoms/how-to-communicate-dementia#content-start.

Alzheimer's Society. "How to Offer Help to Someone With Dementia Who Doesn't Want It," n.d. https://www.alzheimers.org.uk/blog/how-offer-help-someone-dementia-who-doesnt-want-it.

Alzheimer's Society. "Non-verbal Communication and Dementia," January 19, 2022. https://www.alzheimers.org.uk/about-dementia/symptoms-and-diagnosis/symptoms/non-verbal-communication-and-dementia.

Alzheimer Society of Canada. "Making Your Environment Safe," n.d. https://alzheimer.ca/en/help-support/im-caring-person-living-dementia/ensuring-safety-security/making-your-environment-safe.

Alzheimer Society of Canada. "Understanding How Your Relationship May Change," n.d. https://alzheimer.ca/en/help-support/i-have-friend-or-family-member-who-lives-dementia/understanding-how-your-relationship.

Alzheimer's Society. "Reducing and Managing Behaviour That Challenges," August 13, 2021. https://www.alzheimers.org.uk/about-dementia/symptoms-and-diagnosis/symptoms/managing-behaviour-changes.

Alzheimer's Society. "Ten Minutes of Social Interaction Improves Wellbeing in Dementia Care," July 30, 2018. https://www.alzheimers.org.uk/news/2018-07-30/ten-minutes-social-interaction-improves-wellbeing-dementia-care.

Alzheimer's Society. "The Progression and Stages of Dementia." *Factsheet 458LP*, September 2020. https://www.alzheimers.org.uk/sites/default/files/pdf/factsheet_the_progression_of_alzheimers_disease_and_other_dementias.pdf.

Alzheimer's Society. "Understanding and Supporting a Person With Dementia," June 27, 2022. https://www.alzheimers.org.uk/get-support/help-dementia-care/understanding-supporting-person-dementia.

Alzheimer's Society. "Understanding Parts of the Brain," March 18, 2021. https://www.alzheimers.org.uk/about-dementia/symptoms-and-diagnosis/how-dementia-progresses/parts-brain#content-start.

Banovic, Silva, Lejla Junuzovic Zunic, and Osman Sinanovic. "Communication Difficulties as a Result of Dementia." Materia socio-medica, October 2018. https://www.ncbi.nlm.nih.gov/pmc/articles/PMC6195406/.

Berg, Viktor. "How to Cope with the Guilt of Putting Someone in a Care Home." Carehome.co.uk, August 1, 2023. https://www.carehome.co.uk/advice/how-to-cope-with-the-guilt-of-putting-a-loved-one-in-a-care-home.

Cedars-Sinai. "How to Help a Loved One With Alzheimer's or Dementia," n.d. https://www.cedars-sinai.org/blog/how-to-help-a-loved-one-with-alzheimers-or-dementia.html.

Choosing Therapy. "Caregiver Guilt: Causes, Getting Help, & How to Cope," February 16, 2024. https://www.choosingtherapy.com/caregiver-guilt/.

Dementia Australia. "Alcohol Related Dementia," n.d. https://www.dementia.org.au/about-dementia/types-of-dementia/alcohol-related-dementia.

Dementia Australia. "Childhood Dementia," n.d. https://www.dementia.org.au/about-dementia/types-of-dementia/childhood-dementia.

Dementia Australia. "Chronic Traumatic Encephalopathy (CTE) Dementia," n.d. https://www.dementia.org.au/about-dementia/types-of-dementia/chronic-traumatic-encephalopathy-dementia.

Dementia Australia. "Dressing," n.d. https://www.dementia.org.au/support-and-services/families-and-friends/personal-care/dressing.

Dementia Australia. "Frontotemporal Dementia," n.d. https://www.dementia.org.au/information/about-dementia/types-of-dementia/frontotemporal-dementia.

Dementia Australia. "Genetics of Dementia," n.d. https://www.dementia.org.au/information/genetics-of-dementia.

Dementia Australia. "HIV Associated Dementia," n.d. https://www.dementia.org.au/about-dementia/types-of-dementia/aids-related-dementia.

Dementia Australia. "Lewy Body Disease," n.d. https://www.dementia.org.au/about-dementia/types-of-dementia/lewy-body-disease.

Dementia Care Notes. "Improve the Quality of Life of Persons With Dementia | Dementia Care Notes." Dementia Care Notes, India, December 8, 2022. https://dementiacarenotes.in/caregivers/quality-of-life/.

Dementia UK. "Considering a Care Home for a Person With Dementia - Dementia UK," n.d. https://www.dementiauk.org/information-and-support/specialist-diagnosis-and-support/considering-a-care-home-for-a-person-with-dementia/.

Department of Health & Human Services. "Dementia - Communication." Better Health Channel, n.d. https://www.betterhealth.vic.gov.au/health/conditionsandtreatments/dementia-communication.

Department of Health & Human Services, "Dementia - Eating," Better Health Channel, n.d., https://www.betterhealth.vic.gov.au/health/conditionsandtreatments/dementia-eating.

Dev, Hca. "How to Apply for Guardianship of a Parent With Dementia." Stowell Associates, March 9, 2022. https://stowellassociates.com/how-to-get-guardianship-of-parent-with-dementia/.

Dunleavy, Brian P. "Caregiving for Dementia: 8 Key Steps for Care Planning." EverydayHealth.com, November 21, 2022. https://www.everydayhealth.com/dementia/caregiving-for-dementia-key-steps-for-care-planning/.

Family Caregiver Alliance. "Caregiver's Guide to Understanding Dementia Behaviors - Family Caregiver Alliance," March 9, 2024. https://www.caregiver.org/resource/caregivers-guide-understanding-dementia-behaviors/.

Family Caregiver Alliance. "Dementia, Caregiving, and Controlling Frustration - Family Caregiver Alliance," February 4, 2022. https://www.caregiver.org/resource/dementia-caregiving-and-controlling-frustration/.

Family Caregiver Alliance. "Taking Care of YOU: Self-Care for Family Caregivers - Family Caregiver Alliance," January 11, 2023. https://www.caregiver.org/resource/taking-care-you-self-care-family-caregivers/.

Fauth, Elizabeth B., Maria C. Norton, and Jessica J. Weyerman. "Maximizing the Quality of Life for Persons with Dementia." Healthy Aging. Accessed March 13, 2024. https://digitalcommons.usu.edu/cgi/viewcontent.cgi?article=2822&context=extension_curall.

Fewings, Connor. "Dealing With the Guilt of Putting Your Parent in a Nursing Home." First Class Nursing & Care Homes in North Devon and Somerset, April 4, 2018. https://eastleighcarehomes.co.uk/blog/how-to-deal-with-the-guilt-of-putting-your-parent-in-a-nursing-home/#:~:text=how%20you%20feel.-,Dealing%20with%20the%20guilt%20of%20putting%20a%20parent%20in%20a,to%20a%20mental%20health%20professional.

"Five-Star Quality Rating System | CMS," n.d. https://www.cms.gov/medicare/health-safety-standards/certification-compliance/five-star-quality-rating-system.

Gaunt, Angelike. "What to Do When a Parent Is Diagnosed With Dementia: 10 Steps to Help You Move Forward," January 2, 2024. https://www.aplaceformom.com/caregiver-resources/articles/after-dementia-diagnosis.

Hayward, Jack, Charlotte Gould, Emma Palluotto, Emily Kitson, Emily Fisher, and Aimee Spector. "Interventions Promoting Family Involvement With Care Homes Following Placement of a Relative With Dementia: A Systematic Review." *Dementia* 21, no. 2 (December 11, 2021): 618–47. https://doi.org/10.1177/14713012211046595.

Hdoneux, and Hdoneux. "How Do You Convince Your Loved One With Memory Loss to See a Doctor? – Alzheimer's and Dementia Blog – Alzheimers' Association of Northern California and Northern Nevada." *Alzheimer's and Dementia Blog – Alzheimer's Association of Northern California and Northern Nevada* - (blog), January 10, 2019. https://www.alzheimersblog.org/2018/04/27/convince-loved-memory-loss-doctor/.

Healthdirect Australia. "Creating a Calming, Helpful Home for People With Dementia." Healthdirect, n.d. https://www.healthdirect.gov.au/creating-a-calming-home-for-people-with-dementia.

Homage. "How to Convince Your Loved One to Seek Help for Dementia - Homage," May 19, 2022. https://www.homage.sg/resources/how-to-convince-your-loved-one-to-seek-help-for-dementia/.

Home Care Assistance Winnipeg. "Why Nonverbal Communication Is Vital When Caring for Seniors With Dementia," January 21, 2022. https://www.homecareassistancewinnipeg.ca/importance-of-non-verbal-communication-in-dementia-care/.

"How to Help When Dementia Leads to Agitation," n.d. https://www.psychiatry.org/news-room/apa-blogs/how-to-help-when-dementia-leads-to-agitation.

Institute for Healthcare Policy & Innovation. "Dementia's Financial & Family Impact: New Study Shows Outsize Toll," n.d. https://ihpi.umich.edu/news/dementias-financial-family-impact-new-study-shows-outsize-toll.

Koop, Chacour. "Signs It's Time for Memory Care: 13 Questions to Ask," December 19, 2023. https://www.aplaceformom.com/caregiver-resources/articles/is-it-time-for-memory-care.

LCSW, Sarah Cormell. "Finding Balance: Tips for Managing Caregiving and Self-care." Mayo Clinic Health System, June 30, 2023. https://www.mayoclinichealthsystem.org/hometown-health/featured-topic/caregiving-self-care-during-beyond-the-covid-19-pandemic.

Lewis, Kara. "How to Talk to Your Parent About Moving to Memory Care," January 31, 2024. https://www.aplaceformom.com/caregiver-resources/articles/how-to-talk-about-moving-to-memory-care.

Living, Carly Dodd Pacifica Senior. "Touch & Memory Care: The Power Of Touch Therapy for Dementia Residents." *Pacifica Senior Living* (blog), November 2, 2023. https://blog.pacificaseniorliving.com/blog/touch-memory-care-the-power-of-touch-therapy-for-dementia-residents.

Mayo Clinic. "Dementia - Symptoms and Causes - Mayo Clinic," February 13, 2024. https://www.mayoclinic.org/diseases-conditions/dementia/symptoms-causes/syc-20352013.

Moyle, Wendy. "Grand Challenge of Maintaining Meaningful Communication in Dementia Care." *Frontiers in Dementia* 2 (March 3, 2023). https://doi.org/10.3389/frdem.2023.1137897.

Msw, Esther Heerema. "Shadowing in Alzheimer's Disease." Verywell Health, February 10, 2023. https://www.verywellhealth.com/shadowing-in-alzheimers-97620.

Msw, Esther Heerema. "The Benefits of Routines for People With Dementia." Verywell Health, July 29, 2022. https://www.verywellhealth.com/using-routines-in-dementia-97625.

National Institute on Aging. "Tips for Coping With Sundowning," n.d. https://www.nia.nih.gov/health/alzheimers-changes-behavior-and-communication/tips-coping-sundowning#:~:text=Late%20afternoon%20and%20early%20evening,tired%20caregivers%20need%20a%20break.

National Institute on Aging. "What Are Frontotemporal Disorders? Causes, Symptoms, and Treatment," n.d. https://www.nia.nih.gov/health/frontotemporal-disorders/what-are-frontotemporal-disorders-causes-symptoms-and-treatment.

National Institute on Aging. "What Is Lewy Body Dementia? Causes, Symptoms, and Treatments," n.d. https://www.nia.nih.gov/health/lewy-body-dementia/what-lewy-body-dementia-causes-symptoms-and-treatments.

News-Medical. "Childhood Dementia Signs and Symptoms," September 3, 2018. https://www.news-medical.net/health/Childhood-Dementia-Signs-and-Symptoms.aspx.

Palm, Anniina, Risto Vataja, Tiina Talaslahti, Milena Ginters, Hannu Kautiainen, Henrik Elonheimo, Jaana Suvisaari, Nina Lindberg, and Hannu Koponen. 2022. "Incidence and Mortality of Alcohol-Related Dementia and Wernicke-Korsakoff Syndrome: A Nationwide Register Study." *International Journal of Geriatric Psychiatry* 37 (8). https://doi.org/10.1002/gps.5775.

Palmer, Adam. "The Challenges Facing a Family Caregiver." *Senior Living & Nursing Homes in Indiana | ASC* (blog), March 30, 2021. https://www.asccare.com/the-challenges-facing-a-family-caregiver/.

PharmD, Anita Pothen Skaria. "The Economic and Societal Burden of Alzheimer's Disease: Managed Care Considerations." *AJMC*, November 8, 2022. https://www.ajmc.com/view/the-economic-and-societal-burden-of-alzheimer-disease-managed-care-considerations.

"Planning After a Dementia Diagnosis | Alzheimers.gov," n.d. https://www.alzheimers.gov/life-with-dementia/planning-for-future.

"Planning After a Dementia Diagnosis | Alzheimers.gov," n.d. https://www.alzheimers.gov/life-with-dementia/planning-for-future#health-care-planning.

"Planning After a Dementia Diagnosis | Alzheimers.gov," n.d. https://www.alzheimers.gov/life-with-dementia/planning-for-future#long-term-care-planning.

"Positive Aspects of Caregiving." American Psychological Association, 2011. https://www.apa.org/pi/about/publications/caregivers/faq/positive-aspects.

"Positive Aspects of Caregiving." *Https://Www.Apa.Org*, n.d. https://www.apa.org/pi/about/publications/caregivers/faq/positive-aspects.

Professional, Cleveland Clinic Medical. "Caregiver Burnout." Cleveland Clinic, n.d. https://my.clevelandclinic.org/health/diseases/9225-caregiver-burnout.

"Redirect Notice," n.d. https://www.google.com/url?q=https://www.alzheimers.org.uk/get-support/help-dementia-care/understanding-supporting-person-dementia-psychological-emotional-impact%23content-start&sa=D&source=docs&ust=1700597893263681&usg=AOvVaw0v_StyNEDGstR00WZi0yAq.

Reed-Guy, Lauren. "The Stages of Dementia." Healthline, November 27, 2023. https://www.healthline.com/health/dementia/stages#fa-qs.

Samuels, Claire. "Caregiver Statistics: A Data Portrait of Family Caregiving in 2023," June 15, 2023. https://www.aplaceformom.com/senior-living-data/articles/caregiver-statistics.

Schein, Constance, RN. "8 Steps to Advocate for Your Loved One Living With Dementia | Aegis Living." Aegis Living, February 2, 2024. https://www.aegisliving.com/resource-center/advocate-for-your-loved-one-with-dementia/#:~:text=You%20can%20communicate%20their%20vulnerabilities,their%20needs%20are%20being%20met.

Schulz, Richard, Jill Eden, and Committee on Family Caregiving for Older Adults. "Family Caregiving Roles and Impacts." Families Caring for an Aging America - NCBI Bookshelf, November 8, 2016. https://www.ncbi.nlm.nih.gov/books/NBK396398/.

Social Care Institute for Excellence (SCIE). "Dementia - SCIE." SCIE, October 19, 2023. https://www.scie.org.uk/dementia/symptoms/diagnosis/early-diagnosis.asp.

Team, Lifted. "How Do I Tell Family and Friends About a Dementia Diagnosis? - Lifted." Lifted, March 30, 2023. https://www.liftedcare.com/news/how-do-i-tell-family-and-friends-about-a-dementia-diagnosis/.

Tim, Corewood Care, and Tim. "How to Handle Dementia in Loved Ones - Corewood Care." Corewood Care - Home Care & Care Management, May 22, 2023. https://corewoodcare.com/handling-dementia-in-loved-ones/.

UCSF Health. "Self-Care for Caregivers." ucsfhealth.org, May 8, 2023. https://www.ucsfhealth.org/education/self-care-for-caregivers.

USofCare, User. "Listening to Informal Caregivers: Outstanding Challenges and Needs." United States of Care, September 19, 2022. https://unitedstatesofcare.org/listening-to-informal-caregivers-outstanding-challenges-and-needs/.

"Wandering." Alzheimer's Disease and Dementia. Accessed March 13, 2024. https://www.alz.org/help-support/caregiving/stages-behaviors/wandering.

Wang, Yunhe, Moxuan Liu, Qiaoyun Lu, Michael Farrell, Julia Lappin, Jie Shi, Lin Lü, and Yanping Bao. "Global Prevalence and Burden of HIV-associated Neurocognitive Disorder." Neurology 95, no. 19 (November 10, 2020). https://doi.org/10.1212/wnl.0000000000010752.

WebMD. "HIV And AIDS Dementia," December 31, 2006. https://www.webmd.com/hiv-aids/dementia-hiv-infection.

WebMD. "Psychosis: Causes, Symptoms, and Treatment," December 27, 2015. https://www.webmd.com/schizophrenia/what-is-psychosis.

"What Is Dementia and Its Impact on Daily Life as a Carer," n.d. https://www.carersfirst.org.uk/caring-for-someone-with/dementia-how-to-tell-family-and-friends/.

Why touch is important in Alzheimer's care | blog | right at ... Accessed March 13, 2024. https://www.rightathome.net/boston-north/blog/touch-important-in-alzheimers-care.

World Health Organization: WHO and World Health Organization: WHO. "Dementia," March 15, 2023. https://www.who.int/news-room/fact-sheets/detail/dementia.

THE PRACTICAL DEMENTIA CAREGIVER GUIDE

© 2007-2024 AgingCare All Rights Reserved. "7 Signs It's Time for Memory Care," n.d. https://www.agingcare.com/articles/when-is-it-time-to-place-a-loved-one-with-dementia-188309.htm.

Printed in Great Britain
by Amazon